Is Mormonism Christian?

Is Mormonism Christian?

By

Gordon H. Fraser

MOODY PRESS
CHICAGO

Revision of
Is Mormonism Christian?
and
What Does the Book of Mormon Teach?
© 1957, 1964, 1965, 1977 by
THE MOODY BIBLE INSTITUTE
OF CHICAGO

Library of Congress Cataloging in Publication Data

Fraser, Gordon Holmes.
  Is Mormonism Christian?

  A consolidation and revision of the author's 1965 ed.
of Is Mormonism Christian? and 1964 ed. of What does the
Book of Mormon teach?
  Bibliography: p.
    1. Mormons and Mormonism—Controversial literature.
I. Fraser, Gordon Holmes. What does the Book of
Mormon teach? II. Title.
BX8645.F73   230'.9'3   77-6227
ISBN 0-8024-4169-6

Printed in the United States of America

Contents

5

Preface

Two young Mormon missionaries came to my door and introduced themselves as Elders Smith and Jones. They chatted briefly, to put me at ease, before explaining that they represented the Church of Jesus Christ of Latter-Day Saints.

After asking me to what church I belonged, they assured me that this was fine, but that all of the church denominations were wrong because the Church had become apostate soon after the death of the twelve apostles. It was therefore necessary for Christ to restore His Church, which they said had been done when Joseph Smith and five associates established the Church of Jesus Christ in 1830.

They explained that churches today have no prophet, no apostles, and no priesthood with authority to baptize and administer the Holy Spirit with the laying on of hands, as had been done in the early Church. They told how Joseph Smith and his scribe, Oliver Cowdery, had been visited by John the Baptist, who authorized them to baptize each other and then ordained them to the Aaronic priesthood. Later, James, Peter, and John had appeared to them and ordained them to the Melchizedek priesthood.

They explained that the Bible was good (they carried a King James Version of the Bible with them), but

that, in its many translations, it has been corrupted
and is no longer trustworthy. A new record has been
provided: *The Book of Mormon.* This was translated
by their prophet, Joseph Smith, from golden plates
which were revealed by an angel.

They presented a new concept of God. God, they
explained, was an exalted man. They ridiculed the
Christian idea of the Trinity. They said that in his first
vision, Joseph Smith had seen the Father and the Son
as separate physical beings. The Holy Ghost was a
personage of spirit.

They presented a new concept of man. All men,
including Jesus Christ, were spirit beings in a previous life, having been born to heavenly parents, and
are embodied as humans for a period of probation. If
in this probationary period they excel, they will become gods in another life.

In the course of their visit, these young men used
Christian terminology to attack every cardinal doctrine of Christianity. They did so in such a way that an
incautious listener might have been convinced
enough to ask them to return for a second visit.

They gave me some pamphlets and a *Book of Mormon* that had a challenge, or a promise, from the book
on its front endpaper. It read:

> And when you receive these things, I would exhort
> you that you would ask of God, the Eternal Father, in
> the name of Christ, if these things are not true; and if
> ye shall ask with a sincere heart, with real intent,
> having faith in Christ, he will manifest the truth of it
> unto you, by the power of the Holy Ghost (*Book of
> Mormon,* Moroni 10:4-5).

Anyone who has even a basic knowledge of Christian doctrine and a smattering of the history of the Church since Pentecost will recognize the statements of the young missionaries as being untrue. Some of the statements can be attributed to ignorance, others are contrived untruths. Their very presentation betrayed the fact that these young men had been coached in what to say and what not to say.

The Mormon missionaries, and all Mormons, for that matter, insist that they are Christians. They claim to believe in Jesus Christ as Saviour, in the atonement, and in the death and resurrection of Jesus Christ. However, by an examination of their doctrinal writings, we discover that they mean something entirely different from what their terminology would indicate.

That is why this book is being written. Pastors and Christian workers are constantly asking for something that can be used as a guide in dealing with those who are exposed to Mormon indoctrination.

The plan of the book is to deal with each doctrine of Christianity and compare it with the corresponding doctrine of Mormonism. The documentation used is that of the accepted Mormon theologians, the originators of Mormonism, whose writings are considered true. No Mormon will dare to dispute the sayings and writings of their prophets Joseph Smith and Brigham Young. We will use the sacred volumes of Mormonism: *The Book of Mormon, The Doctrine and Covenants, The Pearl of Great Price,* and Joseph Smith's *Inspired Version* of the Bible.

The editions used are indicated in the bibliography. This is important because thousands of

changes have been made in both *The Book of Mormon*
and *The Doctrine and Covenants* since their original
editions. Some of the denominations of Mormonism,
of which there are about twenty still active, do not
accept the teachings of Brigham Young. The Reorganized Church of Jesus Christ of Latter-Day Saints
rejects some of the claimed writings of Joseph Smith,
such as *The Pearl of Great Price* and the last sermon
preached by Joseph Smith at the funeral of King Follett.

We want to call attention to distinctions in doctrine
that, while using similar phraseology, are at opposite
poles. We object to Mormon missionaries posing as
Christians, and our objections are based on the differ-
ences between what they are taught by their General
Authorities and what the Bible teaches.

We would challenge young Mormon missionaries
to take their sacred books—*The Book of Mormon, The
Pearl of Great Price,* and *The Doctrine and
Covenants*—go to the skid rows and ghettos of our
world, and present the Mormon gospel. Let them observe whether the lives of those contacted are transformed to lives of usefulness and joy, as has happened
so often by the power of God through the proclama-
tion of the Christian Gospel.

The Bible and Christianity have been challenged
and examined by malign forces for nearly two
thousand years, without success. The Gospel, as presented in the Bible alone, has consistently been
proved to be the "power of God unto salvation" (Romans 1:16).

1

Missionaries at Your Door

The traditional picture of two young Mormon missionaries coming to your door has been considerably altered. The modern family situation, in which wife and husband are both working, has made it difficult for the missionaries to make satisfactory contacts in house-to-house visitation. The final objectives have not been changed, but the methods have been refined to suit the new family situation.

The new emphasis is to gain the whole family, and the procedure is to arrange for meetings with the entire family present, including the father, who is given the prominent place.

The new manual for missionaries is a masterpiece of organization, patterned after the very best in sales promotion literature. It is entitled *Uniform System for Teaching Families*, and was prepared by the Corporation of the President of the Church of Jesus Christ of Latter-Day Saints, Salt Lake City, in 1973.

The old, colorless, stereotyped, and sometimes boorish presentation of the two-by-two visiting missionaries has given way to a new, more subtle approach. The missionaries ask permission to come in for a visit. If the father is not at home, the callers will attempt to make an appointment for an evening visit and discussion with the entire family present.

When the family is together, the missionaries try to create a friendly situation by urging the youngsters to play their instruments, and by engaging in family singing, storytelling, and recitation. After the desired atmosphere has been created, the leading missionary of the team will engage in a conversational-style presentation of the Mormon message. In their manual, the missionaries are instructed not to deviate from the memorized text and sequence of the arguments until they are completely familiar with them; then they may use their own words to some extent.

Care is taken to present the arguments in such a way as to elicit positive responses. All of the arguments are calculated to get the adult family members to a point of final assent to the teaching being presented. If a negative response is gained, the point is dropped until a time when a favorable response may be expected.

The historic Christian Church, including the family's denomination, is declared to be bankrupt, without an authorized priesthood, and with no apostles or prophets. The doctrine of the Trinity is ridiculed as an artifact of the apostate medieval church conferences. Athanasius is scorned and Arius is eulogized. The need for a prophet with divine authority is emphasized, and Joseph Smith is proposed as the divinely appointed prophet of the Restoration.

The Book of Mormon, supposedly translated from golden plates, is presented as the scriptures of the "new and everlasting covenant" of the Restoration. The "first vision" of the prophet, claimed to have been experienced by Smith when he was fourteen, is given as the source of the Mormon doctrine that the Father and Jesus Christ are two separate gods of flesh and bones, who were once men like ourselves but have been elevated to the status of gods.

An important doctrine of the Mormon church is that all men were preexistent, unembodied spirits before being born as humans in the present state of probation. They insist that men who pass through this period of probation, as men with physical bodies, will become gods in a future life.

In the manual, the missionaries are asked to limit each discussion to forty-five minutes and, of course, to try to obtain consent for a sequence of teaching sessions, until the presentation has advanced to a point where the entire family is ready to submit to baptism. This is the Mormon equivalent to conversion.

There is no presentation of the Lord Jesus as the only Saviour of individual, lost sinners. There is no discussion of the fact that all men are sinners before God and need to experience the new birth. In the Mormon scheme, salvation is progressive and is initiated by baptism by immersion, followed by a lifetime of achievement through good works. The sin problem is taken care of by baptism.

The instruction manual is supplemented by a superbly constructed flip-chart which is held by the missionary who is not leading the discussion. This new device replaces the older flannelgraph method of illustrating the discussion.

The illustrations include beautifully done portraits of the prophet Joseph Smith in various settings that

relate to the key episodes of his life—Smith as a lad,
kneeling in the sacred grove; the angel Moroni ap-
pearing in the prophet's bedroom; Smith and Cowdery being baptized and ordained. There are photo-
graphs of the high officials of the church in several
groupings and of the temples. There is a portrait of
Jesus, shown twice.

The final picture is that of a family group—father,
mother, children, and grandparents—in the heavenly
scene. Here the Mormon imagination flattens out
completely, and the heavenly presentation is that of
uninspired, blank faces, colorless and vacant, floating
along on a nebulous, gray background. They have
never been able to visualize a heavenly scene where
the blessed are more than heavenly unemployed in a
land of eternal sex, and where the sole responsibility
seems to be to propagate spirit children who will
eventually inhabit worlds like ours, in a future state of
probation.

If the contact seems profitless, or the people are
aware of the nature of Mormonism and have a positive
testimony for Jesus Christ and the power of the Gospel, the young missionaries will withdraw.

If the young men get beyond their depth, but the
prospect seems worth promoting further, men of
greater experience and knowledge of the church's
doctrines will follow up the work of the young callers.

It is standard practice for the missionaries to bear
witness to "their assurance that these things are true,
that Joseph Smith is the prophet of God, and the *Book
of Mormon* is the word of God." They will often lay
their hands on their breasts and convey this information with an extremely pious voice. At this point, any

born-again person has a splendid opportunity to witness to the facts of forgiven sins and assurance of salvation here and now. The Mormon can produce no equivalent testimony, and this clear and joyful assurance may give him serious thoughts about the superficiality of his own experience.

2

The Restored Church

One of the most preposterous claims of the Latter-Day Saints is that on April 6, 1830, the true Church of Jesus Christ was reestablished on the earth, after a lapse of seventeen hundred years. In the use of the term "restoration," the Latter-Day saints do not mean reformation, revival, or revitalization; but complete reestablishment, with a restored apostolic authority. According to the Mormons, that authority was forfeited by the apostasy that followed the death of the twelve apostles.

James E. Talmage, one of the most scholarly theologians of the Mormon church, expressed the Latter-Day Saints viewpoint as follows:

> We affirm that with the passing of the so-called apostolic age the church gradually drifted into a condition of apostasy, whereby succession in the priesthood was broken; and that the church, as an earthly organization operating under divine direction and having authority to officiate in spiritual ordinances, ceased to exist.
>
> If therefore the Church of Christ is to be found upon the earth today it must have been reestablished by divine authority; and the holy priesthood must have

16

been restored to the world from which it was lost by
the apostasy of the Primitive Church.[1]

Smith, and his associates, proceeded to "restore" to
the Church a full complement of what he claimed
were the officers of the early Church,—seers, apostles,
elders, bishops, deacons, prophets, and a patriarch.
He arrogated to himself the following posts: "Seer, a
Translator, a Prophet, an Apostle of Jesus Christ, and
Elder of the church through the will of God the Father,
and the grace of your Lord Jesus Christ."[2] The priesthoods, Aaronic and Melchizedek, were added during
the early years of the church, after Sidney Rigdon
became a member of the team.

If Joseph Smith's claim that the "new and everlasting gospel" was restored by this new organization,
the nineteenth century should have been one of the
most spectacular, spiritually, since Pentecost. Let us
examine the facts.

Jesus declared, "Upon this rock [Peter's confession]
I will build my church; and the gates of hell shall not
prevail against it," (Matthew 16:18). If Jesus spoke
with authority, this statement immediately invali-
dates Joseph Smith's argument for restoration.

In His first message in the synagogue in Nazareth,
Jesus declared, "He hath anointed me to preach the
gospel to the poor; he hath sent me to heal the
brokenhearted, to preach deliverance to the captives,
and recovering of sight to the blind, to set at liberty
them that are bruised, to preach the acceptable year of

1. James E. Talmage, *The Great Apostasy: Considered in the Light
   of Scriptural and Secular History*, pp. 18-19.
2. Fawn M. Brodie, *No Man Knows My History: The Life of Joseph
   Smith, the Mormon Prophet*, p. 84.

the Lord" (Luke 4:18-19). Rebuking the Pharisees in
the house of Matthew the publican, Jesus said, "I am
not come to call the righteous, but sinners to repentance" (Matthew 9:13). During His ministry, He
proved His claim to be the Messiah by raising the
dead, cleansing lepers, opening the eyes of the blind,
receiving harlots, thieves, and murderers, and forgiv-
ing sins. When Jesus commissioned His disciples, He
commanded them to preach the Gospel to every creature, to go unto all nations—to the uttermost part of
the earth.

What has the church of the Latter-Day Saints done
to fulfill these basic qualifications of the Church of the
risen Lord Jesus Christ?

They have preached a gospel of doing good works
for salvation, that would immediately disqualify the
sinners to whom Jesus gave forgiveness. They have
consistently avoided preaching to the poor and desti-
tute and have confined their ministry to middle-class
whites. Until recently, they have had no ministry to
prisoners and captives. (They are now attempting
some rehabilitation work among prisoners.) They
have raised no dead nor healed any lepers. They have
not opened the eyes of the blind. (In their hospitals,
they have removed cataracts from the eyes of patients,
but so have doctors who are atheists and Christians.)

They have specifically ruled that harlots and murderers cannot be saved. Neither can apostates from
Mormonism. They have opened no rescue missions,
started no Salvation Armies, founded no refuges for
unwed mothers or centers for the reclamation of dope
addicts and alcoholics. They certainly have not gone
into all the world with their message, for they specifi-

cally avoid going to black races. They have participated in no relief efforts in cases of world disasters:
their vaunted relief program is available only to
Mormons who have kept up their tithing record.

What has the Mormon church done with the tithes
of the faithful, now approaching two million dollars a
day? They finance supermarket chains and the food
processors that supply those chains. They have control of the sugar beet industry of America. They have
purchased automobile factories. They control the
copper producing industry. They control railroads,
paper mills, and a newspaper chain. They have organized insurance companies and savings and loan
associations and have built a financial enclave second
only to the Bank of America. They control the lucra-
tive vice industry of Las Vegas. A count of the Mormon church listings in the Las Vegas telephone direc-
tory numbers more than sixty churches and other
facilities, which means that probably half of the popu-
lation is Mormon, and practically all of the popula-
tion of Las Vegas is directly or indirectly engaged in
work related to the vice industry.

By contrast, in the years since Joseph Smith went
treasure hunting, found golden plates, and pretended
to translate *The Book of Mormon*, what has the *real*
Church of Jesus Christ been doing?

While Joseph Smith was hunting buried treasure,
Robert Morrison was finishing his life's work of translating the Bible into the Chinese language.

While Smith was translating *The Book of Mormon*,
another New Englander, Adoniram Judson, was
translating the Bible into the Burmese language.

While Henry Harmon Spalding was translating the

gospel of Matthew into the language of the Nez Percés
Indians, Smith was putting the finishing touches on
The Pearl of Great Price and pretending to translate
the Book of Abraham from Egyptian papyri, a now
well-established fraud.

While James Evans was translating the Bible into
the Cree language and creating his own syllabic script
to do so, Smith was writing his *King Follett Discourse*,
which involved the Mormon church, for all time, in
the doctrine that God was once a man.

While David Livingstone was pushing into the
heart of Africa with the Gospel of Jesus Christ, and
Hudson Taylor was pressing into inland China with
the same message, Brigham Young was taking his
Mormon followers to the mountainous West and establishing his Mormon empire.

While Brigham Young was reddening the soil of
Utah with the blood of apostates and gentiles in pur-
suance of his "blood atonement doctrine," William
Booth was establishing his worldwide Salvation
Army to rescue thousands from the quicksands of vice
and crime in the world's great cities.

While President John Taylor was fighting to preserve the plural marriage doctrine of the Mormon
church, a thousand rescue missions were being operated throughout the United States and Great Britain.

What is the great difference between the highly
successful, soul-saving mission of the Church of the
Lord Jesus, against which He said the gates of hell
would not prevail, and the ponderous establishment
of the Mormon church, which can point to no lives
transformed by the Gospel? Joseph Smith's gospel has
no cure for sin and no power to weld together a living

body of believers.

The Mormon church boasts nearly thirty-five thousand missionaries in the field, with a worldwide membership of three million. The Church of the living Lord Jesus, in the same life span, has added multiplied millions to the Body of Christ. God does the counting in His Church.

3

The First Vision

Latter-Day Saints build the entire structure of their doctrines that God is an exalted man and that there is a plurality of gods on a vision which Joseph Smith claimed to have had. This is known as the "first vision." In all official literature of the church, it is dated at 1820, when Joseph was in his fifteenth year. In this vision, he claimed that the Father and the Son appeared to him and gave him the first intimation of the ministries he would eventually perform.

There was a crisis in Smith's experience that led to this spiritual exercise. It was the occasion of revival meetings being held in his home area. The meetings fanned the populace into such interest that many local churches were gaining adherents. Smith recorded the events as follows:

> Some time in the second year after our removal to Manchester, there was in the place where we lived an unusual excitement on the subject of religion. It commenced with the Methodists, and soon became general among all the sects in that region of country. Indeed, the whole district of country seemed affected by it, and great multitudes united themselves to the different religious parties, which created no small stir

and division amongst the people, some crying, "Lo, here!" and others, "Lo, there!" Some were contending for the Methodist faith, some for the Presbyterian, and some for the Baptist. . . . I was at that time in my fifteenth year. My father's family was proselyted to the Presbyterian faith, and four of them joined that church.[1]

Joseph claimed to be greatly disturbed by all of the commotion and resolved to seek guidance. He had read, in James 1:5, "If any of you lack wisdom, let him ask of God, that giveth to all men liberally, and upbraideth not; and it shall be given him." He came to a decision and later recorded it.

At length I came to the conclusion that I must either remain in darkness and confusion, or else I must do as James directs, that is, ask of God. . . . So, in accordance with this, my determination to ask of God, I retired to the woods to make the attempt. . . . It was the first time in my life that I had made such an attempt, for amidst all my anxieties I had never as yet made the attempt to pray vocally.[2]

At that moment, Joseph claimed, he was clutched by a power that made him speechless and a "thick darkness" gathered around him.

Just at this moment of great alarm, I saw a pillar of light exactly over my head, above the brightness of the sun, which descended gradually until it fell upon me. It no sooner appeared than I found myself delivered from the enemy which held me bound. When the light rested upon me I saw two Personages, whose

1. Joseph Smith, *The Pearl of Great Price*, Joseph Smith 2:5, 7.
2. Ibid., 2:13-14.

brightness and glory defy all description, standing
above me in the air. One of them spake unto me,
calling me by name and said, pointing to the other—
This is My Beloved Son, Hear Him!

My object in going to inquire of the Lord was to
know which of all the sects was right, that I might
know which to join. . . . I was answered that I should
join none of them, for they were all wrong; and the
personage who addressed me said that all their creeds
were an abomination in his sight; that these professors were all corrupt; that: "they draw near to me with
their lips, but their hearts are far from me."[3]

The experience, as told above, establishes two of
the principles upon which the Mormon church is
built: (1) that the whole church was corrupt and apostate and needed a restoration, and (2) that the theism
of the new church would be built on the principle of a
plurality of gods.

Regarding this first vision, David O. McKay, a recent president of the church, says, "The appearance
of the Father and the Son to Joseph Smith is the
foundation of the church."[4]

Another president of the church, Joseph Fielding
Smith, wrote, "The greatest event that has ever occurred in the world since the resurrection of the Son
of God . . . was the coming of the Father and the Son to
that boy, Joseph Smith."[5]

LeGrand Richards, a presiding bishop of the
Church of Jesus Christ of Latter-Day Saints, wrote,
"On the morning of the beautiful spring day in 1820

---

3. Ibid., 2:16-17.
4. David O. McKay, *Gospel Ideals,* p. 85.
5. Joseph Fielding Smith, *Gospel Doctrine,* p. 495.

there occurred one of the most important and momentous events in the world's history. God, the Eternal Father and his Son, Jesus Christ, appeared to Joseph Smith and gave instructions concerning the establishment of the kingdom of God upon the earth in these latter days."[6] He said also, "The visit of the Father and the Son to Joseph Smith . . . was the greatest event of the nineteenth century."[7]

What are the facts regarding the "first vision" and the doctrines that are based on it? Unfortunately, the three churchmen named above wrote their dogmatic statements before the present pack of nasty gentile, apostate Mormon, and realistic Mormon researchers became so successful in digging up the older records. Paul Cheesman is a researcher who has discovered some rather startling inconsistencies in the record.

The story of the first vision, as it is given today in *The Pearl of Great Price*, was not written by Joseph Smith until 1838, eighteen years after the supposed event, and not published until 1842, in *Times and Seasons*, twenty-two years after the event.

Anyone reading Joseph Smith's story in its final form will detect a number of internal inconsistencies that indicate changes made in the doctrines of the church and in the mind of Joseph Smith as time went on. Unfortunately, too, these evidences are in solid print.

The church writers have committed themselves to the dates given by Smith in the final story. There he says the event happened when he was in his fifteenth year, which was 1820. However, the circumstance

6. LeGrande Richards, *A Marvelous Work and a Wonder*, p. 6.
7. Ibid., p. 13.

sending Joseph to the sacred grove was the upsetting revival meetings being held in Palmyra. Through the research of the Reverend Wesley P. Walters, we discover that there were no revival meetings until the fall of 1824, when Joseph would have been nearly nineteen years old. This would also place the first vision a year *after* his first visit from the angel Moroni, which Smith dates as September 21, 1823. The records of the three churches mentioned by Joseph show the years 1820-23 as completely sterile years, the Presbyterians reporting "no revivals," the Baptists reporting a gain of only six members, and the Methodist church showing a loss of forty-six members in the district.[8]

Oliver Cowdery, Smith's intimate associate who aided in compiling a record of Joseph's early years, places the revival in 1823. That was the year Joseph received his first visit from Moroni and was told about the golden plates.[9]

Some dates may be unimportant, but such an important event as a visit from the Father and the Son would certainly be firmly impressed on the mind of a person fourteen or eighteen years old. It would be too dramatic an event to be misdated or forgotten by the one to whom it happened in a mere eighteen years or less.

More important are the doctrinal implications of the vision. By 1838, when Joseph Smith finalized his statement, the doctrine of the anthropomorphic god and the plurality of gods was firmly fixed in his mind and in the doctrines of the church. But this was not so in 1830 or in 1835.

8. Wesley P. Walters, *New Light on Mormon Origins*, p. 12.
9. Ibid.

In 1830, *The Book of Mormon* reflected a reasonably orthodox concept of God, as presented in the Bible. In 1835, Smith and his associates were delivering their "Lectures on Faith" in the Kirtland Temple. In lecture 5, Smith says,

> There are two personages who constitute the great, matchless, governing, and supreme power over all things, by whom all things were created and made, that are created and made, whether visible or invisible, whether in heaven, on earth, or in the earth, under the earth, or throughout the immensity of space. They are the Father and the Son—the Father being a personage OF SPIRIT, glory, and power, possessing all perfection and fullness, the Son, who is in the bosom of the Father, a personage of tabernacle, made or fashioned like unto man, or being in the form and likeness of man, or rather man was formed after his likeness and in his image; he is also the express image and likeness of the personage of the Father, possessing all the fullness of the Father. . . .
>
> And he being the only begotten of the Father, full of grace and truth, and having overcome received a fullness of glory of the Father, possessing the same mind with the Father, whose mind is the Holy Spirit, that bears record of the Father and the Son, and these three are one; or in other words, these three constitute the great matchless, governing and supreme, power over all things; by whom all things were created and made, and these three constitute the Godhead, and are one. . . . From the foregoing account of the Godhead . . . the saints have a sure foundation laid for the exercise of faith unto life and salvation, through the atonement and mediation of Jesus Christ; by whose blood they have a forgiveness of sin.[10]

10. Joseph Smith, "Lectures on Faith," *Doctrine and Covenants* (1890 ed.), p. 55.

This and a whole series of lectures are included in the earlier editions of *The Doctrine and Covenants*, including the 1918 edition. They are no longer included because this is not the present Mormon doctrine of the Father and the Son, and apparently was not Smith's concept when he was reporting his vision in 1838.

It is also disconcerting that the two personages of the Father and the Son are not reported in any of the literature until that time. There are three handwritten reports on the first vision, but all are different. References vary concerning angels, a visitation of angels, a personage, two personages, and the Lord Jesus.

If Smith had a vision in 1820, or 1824, it certainly had no important effect on his life. In the years between 1820 and 1826, during which he reports several contacts with an angel, Smith was engaged in various trivial pursuits, including treasure hunting by means of a "seer-stone." This led to his arrest, trial, and conviction as a "glass-looker." Obviously there is nothing villainous about treasure hunting. But Smith apparently was accepting fees for his services. No treasure was ever found—except the golden plates.

It would seem that Joseph Smith built up his doctrinal views to such a point that the first vision of the Father and the Son became necessary documentation for his doctrine.

4

The Mormon Genealogy
of Gods and Men

Joseph Smith's writings declare that "Man was in
the beginning with God." It is very important to understand the implications of this concept: out of it
comes the teaching concerning spirit children, men,
and gods. In order to study this teaching, we will
begin with ourselves. According to Mormon teaching, we are here in mortal bodies for a period of
probation. At the end of that period, at physical death,
we will arise as physical-spiritual beings to enter into
an enlarged sphere of existence in which we shall
become gods. Before receiving these mortal bodies,
we were spirit beings. We are not created spirits, but
spirits born by procreation of a heavenly father and
mother.[1] Our heavenly parents are gods because they,
too, passed through a phase of spirit-beings, born into
physical, mortal bodies, to experience a period of
probation. They, too, became gods as they progressed
successfully out of their earthly probation. Their parents also passed this way, and so on back, ad infinitum, to whatever personages constituted the "beginning."

1. Milton R. Hunter, *The Gospel Through the Ages*, pp. 98-99.

When humans achieve godhood, a man and his wife/wives will produce an infinite number of spirit children. They will become a heavenly father and mother. Their spirit children will eventually complete the cycle by being given mortal bodies for their period of probation. The process will continue to infinity in cycles: spirits, mortal bodies in probation, physical death leading to resurrection, spiritual-physical personages, godhood.

Mormon teachers have been quite vocal in declaring this principle. Orson Pratt, who was considered by the early Mormons to be their most learned scholar, wrote,

> The Gods who dwell in the heavens . . . have been redeemed from the grace in a world which existed before the foundation of the earth was laid. They and the heavenly body which they now inhabit were once in a fallen state . . . they were exalted also, from fallen men to Cellestial Gods to inhabit their heaven forever and ever.[2]

> We were begotten by our Father in Heaven; the person of our Father in Heaven was begotten in a previous heavenly world by his Father; and again, he was begotten by a still more ancient father; and so on, from generation to generation, from one heavenly world to another still more ancient, until our minds are wearied and lost in the multiplicity of generations and successive worlds, and as a last resort, we wonder in our minds, how far back the genealogy extends, and how the first world was formed and the first Father was begotten.[3]

The idea of a heavenly mother as well as a heavenly

2. Orson Pratt, *The Seer,* p. 22.
3. Ibid., p. 132.

father will appear logical if we accept the Mormon concept of the procreation of intelligent spirit personages, who will eventually receive mortal bodies such as we inhabit. Bruce McConkie, a member of the First Council of the Seventy, writes,

> Implicit in the Christian verity that all men are the spirit children of an Eternal Father is the usually unspoken truth that they are also the offspring of an Eternal Mother. An exalted and glorified Man of Holiness could not be a father unless a woman of like glory, perfection, and holiness was associated with Him as a mother. The begetting of children makes a man a father and a woman a mother whether we are dealing with man in his mortal or immortal state.[4]

Milton R. Hunter, a contemporary Mormon theologian who readily accepts the old pagan philosophers as good documentation, writes,

> The stupendous truth of the existence of a Heavenly Mother, as well as a Heavenly Father, became established facts in Mormon theology. A complete realization that we are the offspring of Heavenly Parents— that we were begotten and born into the spirit world and grew to maturity in that realm—becomes an integral part of Mormon philosophy. Those verities are basic in the Gospel plan of eternal progression.[5]

One should keep in mind the above teaching of continuous progression to godhood and compare this with the Christian doctrines of the deity of Christ, the problem of sin and salvation, and the many statements of Scripture with regard to man's origin from the hand of God and his destiny in the eternal presence of God.

---

4. Bruce McConkie, *Mormon Doctrine*, p. 516.
5. Hunter, pp. 98-99.

5

The Gods of the Mormons

The first item in the Mormon doctrinal statement, first published in 1838, states, "We believe in God, the Eternal Father, and in His son Jesus Christ, and in the Holy Ghost."[1] At first glance this would seem to be a completely acceptable trinitarian declaration of belief, and there is no doubt but that the wording was given so as to impress the casual inquirer with the orthodoxy of the new church. Many people hearing or reading this statement are favorably impressed by it and come to the conclusion that the Mormons are just another branch of Christianity—somewhat different, but rather successful.

Before accepting the Mormon doctrinal statement regarding the nature of Deity, we are justified in asking for some definitions to see if the statement really means what it seems to mean from the biblical viewpoint.

The god of Mormon theology is not the God of the Bible or of evangelical Christianity. We may go further and say that the present Mormon concepts of god as an exalted man and of the plurality of gods are totally absent from *The Book of Mormon.*

1. Joseph Smith, *Pearl of Great Price,* Articles of Faith, p. 59.

The names of god as used in *The Book of Mormon* are scarcely different from those used in the King James Version of the Bible: Joseph Smith and his coauthors quoted copiously from it while composing their volume of Mormon belief. When Smith was writing *The Book of Mormon*, with the assistance of Oliver Cowdery and Martin Harris (and, we suspect, Sidney Rigdon), he and his associates had no greater knowledge of the names and attributes of God than the average person of their day.

There was little Bible exposition available to them in the back country of upper New York State: the preachers of the area were camp meeting exhorters who themselves knew little of the plan or structure of the Scriptures. Calvinism and Arminianism, election and freewill, were discussed about as intelligently by the tavern keepers as they were by the religious-minded. But the teaching of the grace of God in salvation was not being taught by the Calvinists, nor was holy living being practiced, except spasmodically, by the Arminians. Because there was no knowledge of dispensational teaching, instructions given by the prophets to Israel in the Old Testament had no distinction from the teachings of Paul to the young churches in Asia Minor and Europe. A quotation from the Bible was equally valid if it was the saying of Satan or Isaiah. The good went to heaven, and the bad went to hell, depending upon their status at the moment of death.

The new church of Alexander Campbell,* the ad-

---

* Alexander Campbell's Church of Christ is important because Sidney Rigdon, who masterminded the doctrines of the Latter-Day Saints, was a long-time associate of Campbell's.

ventist groups of William Miller, and the spiritism of
the Fox Sisters all grew out of this soil. Out of this
same seedbed came *The Book of Mormon*, claiming
to be a divine revelation but bearing all of the marks
of a forgery by an ignorant but highly imaginative
and precocious youth. Joseph Smith's scribe was
Oliver Cowdery, who doubled as a schoolteacher
and a blacksmith. A local farmer, Martin Harris, who
was generally successful in business but was a cred-
ulous visionary in religious matters, was important
to the project because he had the resources to finance
it.

The person of Deity depicted in *The Book of Mormon* was created by an uninstructed religionist, who
acknowledged the fact of God as presented by the
"exhorters" simply because he did not wish to pose
as an atheist. God is taken for granted. No discernment is exercised in the use of the several biblical
names of God. *The Eternal God* is used interchange-
ably with the *Messiah*. *The Most High* is used in
connection with Jews,† and *Jehovah*, with Gentiles.‡

The following examples show this inconsistency.
In Mosiah 3:18 (124 B.C.), we find "The Atoning blood
of Christ, the Lord Omnipotent." The term "atoning
blood of Christ," is out of time sequence in 124 B.C.
Besides, it is nonscriptural and doctrinally incorrect.
The only time the word *atonement* is used in con-
nection with the work of Christ is in Romans 5:11
(KJV), and here it should have been translated

---

†In the King James Version of the Bible, the term *The Most High*
was always used by the Gentiles, and by the Semites only for its
poetic value.
‡The terms *Jehovah* and *Elohim* were used uniformly by Semites
and, later, Jews.

"reconciliation." In the Old Testament, the term *atonement* is used constantly and implies the covering of sin by the blood of animal sacrifices. The New Testament uses the term *redemption*, which has to do with the payment for sin as provided in the work of Christ on Calvary. The Latin term *omnipotent* would hardly have been used by the natives of America in 124 B.C.

In 1 Nephi, chapters 11-14, we find the term "the Lamb of God." It is used forty-six times, with eight variations. In Scripture, the term is peculiar to the writings of the apostle John and would be completely out of time sequence in 600 B.C. Joseph Smith probably was not conscious of having or not having a definable concept of God while writing *The Book of Mormon.* However, as soon as his new church started to take form, it was necessary for him to develop a theism to fit its doctrine.

By this time Sidney Rigdon, who had been disfellowshipped by both the Baptists and Alexander Campbell's new church,[2] had joined ranks with Smith. There is no evidence that Rigdon was a competent theologian. Certainly his knowledge of the text of the Bible was not coupled with any evidence of spiritual discernment. He was merely a religious experimenter who saw in Smith's new religion an opportunity to make a place for himself. Without doubt, much of Smith's new theology and practically all of the religious phraseology of his books show Rigdon's influence.

Following the publication of *The Book of Mormon,*

2. Fawn M. Brodie, *No Man Knows My History: The Life of Joseph Smith, the Mormon Prophet,* pp. 94-95.

Smith's ideas developed rapidly. A thoroughly corporeal god emerged as the doctrines and covenants
started to accumulate and as the *Inspired Version*§ of
the Bible was prepared. By the time *The Pearl of Great
Price* was finished, Smith's concept was that of a
plurality of gods. By the end of his short lifetime,
when he delivered the King Follett Discourse,[3] God
was one of many gods, and Adam was the god of this
world. The gods were exalted men, and men had
become incipient gods. Smith's theism had become
polytheism.

With the raw material of Smith's writings available,
it was easy for the followers of the prophet, Brigham
Young, Orson and Parley Pratt, and others, to develop
the present, unbiblical doctrine of deity. The Mormons may be quite sincere in their belief in their god,
but he is not the God of the Bible.

A few samples of the evolution of Smith's theism
will be quite enlightening. Three in particular, from
The Book of Mormon, will suffice to demonstrate that
Smith's early concept of God was not particularly
unorthodox; it was just inherited. In 1830, when he
was writing *The Book of Mormon*, he said,

> For I know that God is not a partial God, neither a
> changeable being: But He is unchangeable from all
> eternity to all eternity.[4]

§ Soon after the completion of *The Book of Mormon*, Joseph
Smith and his scribes made a revision of the Bible that is
generally referred to as the *Inspired Version*. It added to the
Scriptures the text needed to support Smith's new doctrines.
3. A funeral sermon expounding the new anthropomorphic God
concept. Published by the church from time to time and more
recently in *Ensign*, April and May issues, 1971.
4. Joseph Smith, *The Book of Mormon*, Moroni 8:18.

> And Zeezrom said unto him: "Thou sayest that
> there is a true and living God?" And Amulek said:
> "Yea, there is a true and living God." Now Zeezrom
> said: "Is there more than one God?" And he
> answered, "No!"[5]

> For do we not read that God is the same yesterday,
> today, and forever, and in him there is no variableness
> neither shadow of changing? And now if ye have
> imagined up unto yourselves a god who doth vary . . .
> then have ye imagined up unto yourselves a god who
> is not a God of miracles. . . . I say unto you he changeth
> not; if so he would cease to be God.[6]

We cannot help but believe that Mormon had in his
hands the King James Version of Hebrews 13:8 and
James 1:17, and that the date was 1830 instead of the
fourth century A.D.

The early "revelations" recorded in *The Doctrine
and Covenants* were contemporary with the publication of *The Book of Mormon*. In them, the concept of
God had not changed particularly. In 1830, he wrote,

> By these things we know that there is a God in
> heaven, who is infinite and eternal, from everlasting
> to everlasting the same unchangeable God, the framer
> of heaven and earth . . . [he] gave unto them com-
> mandments that they should love and serve him, the
> only living and true God.[7]

Note, by contrast, the evolution of the concept of
God in the first thirteen years of the church's history.
In 1843, Smith wrote,

5. Ibid., Alma 11:26-29.
6. Ibid., Mormon 9:9-10, 19.
7. Joseph Smith, *The Doctrine and Covenants*, 20:17-18.

The Father has a body of flesh and bones as tangible
as man's; the Son also.[8]

Then shall they be gods, because they have all
power, and the angels are subject unto them.[9]

By the time Joseph Smith prepared *The Pearl of
Great Price,* he had started a study of the Hebrew
language. He was never more than a word-dropper in
Hebrew, but he learned enough to season his writings
and speeches with allusions to it.

He discovered that the term *Elohim,* by which we
are introduced to God in Genesis 1, is in the plural
form and was used by later writers and nonbiblical
writers to express the idea of many gods. He grasped
this fact as the final documentation on which to base
his "plurality of gods" doctrine. In the Book of Abraham, he used the term "the Gods" to translate the
Hebrew *Elohim* in his paraphrase of Genesis 1.

The final step downward in Smith's theism is well
expressed in his discourse at the funeral of Elder King
Follett. This discourse was delivered before an audi-
ence of twenty thousand and was reported by four
scribes: Willard Richards, Wilford Woodruff, Thomas
Bullock, and William Clayton. It was delivered in
April, 1844. Smith was murdered on June 27, 1844,
and the King Follett Discourse was published in the
August 1, 1844, edition of *Times and Seasons.*[10]

Chaos resulted from Smith's death. Therefore it is
unlikely that the council of the twelve would have
had time or inclination to manufacture a document so

8. Ibid., 130:22.
9. Ibid., 132:20.
10. Early publication of the Latter-Day Saints that served as their
    official voice.

unrelated to the stupendous problems that confronted them.

Mormon theologians have used the *King Follett Discourse* as Smith's final word on the doctrines of God and man. The following excerpt is from it.

> I am going to inquire after God: for I want you all to know him and be familiar with him. . . . I will go back to the beginning before the world was, to show you what kind of a being God is.
>
> God was once as we are now, and is an exalted man, and sits enthroned in yonder heavens. . . . I say, if you were to see him today, you would see him like a man in form—like yourselves in all the person, image, and very form of a man.
>
> I am going to tell you how God came to be God. We have imagined and supposed that God was God from all eternity. I will refute that idea, and take away the veil, so that you may see.
>
> It is the first principle of the gospel to know for certainty the character of God and to know that we may converse with him as one man with another, and that he was once a man like us; yea, that God himself, the father of us all, dwelt on an earth, the same as Jesus Christ did.
>
> What did Jesus say? . . . The scripture informs us that Jesus said, "as the Father hath power to himself, even so hath the Son power" . . . to do what? Why, what the Father did. The answer is obvious—in a manner to lay down his body and take it up again.
>
> Here then, is eternal life—to know the only wise and true God; and you have got to learn how to be Gods yourselves, and to be kings and priests to God, the same as all Gods have done before you, namely, by going from one small degree to another, and from a small capacity to a great one; from grace to grace, from

exaltation to exaltation, until you attain to the resurrection of the dead, and are able to dwell in the everlasting burnings, and to sit in glory, as do those who sit enthroned in everlasting power.[11]

Many of the apostles of Joseph Smith, particularly those who followed Brigham Young to Utah, have written and lectured on Smith's concept of God, and, while these are not considered "inspired" by the church, they are considered authoritative. Much has been written by the several presidents of the church to confirm Smith's doctrines. The presidency of the Mormon church carries with it the power to receive "revelations," having as much authority as the Romanists claim for the pope when he speaks ex cathedra. Therefore we may take these utterances as being the authoritative teachings of the Mormons. Here are some samples.

In the beginning the head of the Gods called a council of the Gods; and they came together and concocted a plan to create and populate the world and people it.[12]

Remember that God our heavenly Father was perhaps once a child and mortal like we are, and rose step by step in the scale of progress, in the school of advancement; has moved forward and overcome until he has arrived at the point where he now is.[13]

Mormon prophets have continuously taught the sublime truth that God the Eternal Father was once a mortal man who passed through a school of earth

11. Joseph Smith, *King Follett Discourse*, pp. 8-10.
12. Joseph Smith, in *Journal of Discourses* 6:5.
13. Orson Hyde, in *Journal of Discourses* 6:123.

similar to that through which we are passing. He
became God—an exalted being.[14]

Mormonism does not tend to debase God to the
level of man, but to exalt man to the perfection of
God.[15]

This last utterance coincides perfectly with Satan's
statement to Eve in the Garden of Eden when he said,
"Ye shall be as gods" (Genesis 3:5). Satan said it long
before Joseph Smith said it.

It is quite obvious that Joseph Smith's concept of
God followed the deterioration pattern of the Gentile
God-concept as outlined by the apostle Paul in Ro-
mans 1:21-26.

Because that, when they knew God, they glorified
him not as God, neither were thankful; but became
vain in their imaginations, and their foolish heart was
darkened. Professing themselves to be wise, they became fools, and changed the glory of the uncorruptible God into an image made like to corruptible man,
and to birds, and fourfooted beasts, and creeping
things. Wherefore God also gave them up to unclean-
ness through the lusts of their own hearts, to dishon-
our their own bodies between themselves: who
changed the truth of God into a lie, and worshipped
and served the creature more than the Creator, who is
blessed for ever. Amen. For this cause God gave them
up unto vile affections.

Paul's implication is that a pattern of deterioration in
morals parallels the deteriorating concept of God.
Note the sequence in Paul's formula: (1) they knew
God, but worshiped Him not as God, (2) their foolish

14. Milton R. Hunter, *The Gospel Through the Ages*, p. 104.
15. Charles Penrose, *Millennial Star* 23:181.

heart was darkened, (3) professing themselves to be wise, they became fools, (4) they changed the glory of the uncorruptible God into the likeness of corruptible man, and so (5) God gave them up to vile passions.

In Paul's scale of deterioration, one can easily detect the point at which man equates his human reason with the thoughts of God. At that point, the anthropomorphic god emerges.

In the history of Mormonism, the doctrines of God as being an exalted man and of man being a potential god developed in 1830-31. It was during this same period that charges and countercharges of adultery and polygamy were being heard and vigorously denied by the church.[16]

In the histories of the world's pagan religions, three developments usually occur coincidentally: (1) the emergence of a physical god, such as the frivolous and carnal Zeus of the Greeks; (2) the deification of man, usually ending in ancestor worship; and (3) the acceptance of sexual irregularities as acts of worship. This is what Paul is saying in the Romans letter, and this, in pattern if not in detail, is what happened in the development of Joseph Smith's theism.

The Book of Mormon was published early in 1830, and on April 6 of that year, the church was founded. Within a matter of months, a coterie of religionists emerged and began to formulate the doctrines and practices of the new church. Of the five men contributing to the pool of religious knowledge, only one, Sidney Rigdon, had had any ministerial training and experience. He had been expelled from Alexander

16. Brodie, pp. 184-85, 246, 307.

Campbell's restoration movement because of his erratic beliefs and behavior. Rigdon brought with him some of Campbell's doctrines and most of the ecclesiology from his former connection and is responsible, according to David Whitmer, one of the cofounders, for the Mormon system of priesthood.

By August, the new concept of the physical nature of God was beginning to show itself. The Mormons consider Michael to be a god, grouped in a triad consisting of Elohim, Jehovah, and Michael. In a revelation, given as Section 27 in *Doctrine and Covenants*, Michael is equated with "Adam, the father of all" and is called the "Prince of all, the Ancient of Days."[17] According to a revelation dated March, 1832, "Michael your Prince"[18] was given the keys of salvation. At least six other references in *The Doctrine and Covenants* established this Adam-Michael equation. Thus, since Michael is made to be one of the gods, and Michael became Adam, Adam must have been the incarnation of a god.

A definitive statement, made by Milton R. Hunter, a contemporary Mormon teacher and writer, sums up the concept of men becoming gods and gods advancing to greater perfection.

THE PERSONALITY OF GOD

We accept the fact that God is the Supreme Intelligent Being in the universe. He has the greatest knowledge, the most perfect will, and the most infinite power of any person within the realm of our understanding. To us, His love, His justice, His mercy, and His control over the universe are all infinite. We know

---

17. Joseph Smith, *Doctrine and Covenants*, 27:11.
18. Ibid., 78:16.

that God absolutely transcends the finite understanding of mortals. He possesses all the virtues that mankind possesses in such an enhanced degree that when we attempt to define Him we fail, because He is infinitely greater than the most complete picture that mortals can give of Him.

HOW HE BECAME GOD

Yet, if we accept the great law of eternal progression, we must accept the fact that there was a time when Deity was much less powerful than He is today. Then how did He become glorified and exalted and attain His present status of Godhood? In the first place, aeons ago God undoubtedly took advantage of every opportunity to learn the laws of truth and as He became acquainted with each new verity He righteously obeyed it. From day to day He exerted His will vigorously, and as a result became thoroughly acquainted with the forces lying about Him. As He gained more knowledge through persistent effort and continuous industry, as well as through absolute obedience, His understanding of the universal laws continued to become more complete. Thus He grew in experience and continued to grow until He attained the status of Godhood. In other words, He became God by absolute obedience to all the truth, and thereby became the author of eternal truth. Therefore, the road that the Eternal Father followed to Godhood was one of living at all times a dynamic, industrious, and completely righteous life. There is no other way to exaltation.[19]

The writer has asked a number of Mormons of high standing if they believe Hunter's statement. They have replied, "Why, certainly! How else can we achieve exaltation?"

19. Hunter, pp. 114-15.

We do not deny the right of the Mormons to worship such a god if they wish. But that is not the God of the Bible and true Christianity.

Two books which present the true Christian concept of God are *The Knowledge of the Holy,* by A. W. Tozer (New York: Harper & Row, 1975) and *Knowing God,* by J. I. Packer (Downers Grove, Ill.: Inter-Varsity, 1973). We recommend these to you.

6

The Adam-God Doctrine

A few of our critics have objected to our using Brigham Young's statement that Adam is "the only God with whom we have to do." Modern exponents of Mormonism will insist that the Adam-God doctrine was never taught and is not taught today. They will say, with their former president Joseph Fielding Smith, that Young's statement was "in all probability . . . erroneously transcribed."[1]

The statement probably was correctly transcribed and meant just what Brigham Young intended it to mean. Certainly the doctrine was taught long before Young enunciated it so forcibly. The polygamous branch of the Utah church (the fundamentalists) defended the doctrine vigorously.[2]

The whole system of Mormon teaching— (1) that there are many gods, (2) that all gods are exalted men, (3) that men may become gods, (4) and that men are embodied spirits that were born of god-parents in a previous existence—requires that at some point in the cycle Adam must become a god.

The Mormon theologians have a distinct problem at this point. Joseph Smith and Brigham Young postu-

---

1. Joseph Fielding Smith, *Gospel Doctrine*, p. 96.
2. W. Gordon Hackney, *That Adam-God Doctrine*.

lated a trinity of three separate gods who collabo-
rated in the organizing and populating of this earth.
They name the three, in the temple ritual and
throughout their literature, as Elohim, Jehovah, and
Michael. They have rank, Elohim being the highest.
Probably neither Smith nor Young had read their
Bibles sufficiently to know that Elohim and Jehovah
are the same Person. They could have read in
Deuteronomy 6:4, "Hear, O Israel, Jehovah our
Elohim is One Jehovah." Or they could have noted
that it was the person of Jehovah Elohim who made
man in His image (Genesis 2:7). They did not know
that Michael was neither a god nor a man but was,
rather, a powerful, created, spirit being, who, with
Gabriel, was a messenger of God to man on a number
of recorded occasions. Never was he a god; he was
only a servant. He has not been and never will be
embodied as a man.

Joseph Smith and his followers have a difficult
problem in postulating the original god, "Head of the
Gods," as Joseph Smith describes Him.[3] If all gods are
exalted men and all men are potential gods, where did
it start?

Parley Pratt, one of the men who formulated Mormon doctrine, gives the following definitive statement:

> Gods, angels and men are all of the same species,
> one race, one great family ... the great distinguishing
> difference between one portion of the race and
> another consists in the varied grades of intelligence
> and purity ... in the series of progressive being.[4]

3. Joseph Smith, in *Journal of Discourses* 6:5.
4. Parley P. Pratt, *Key to the Science of Theology*, pp. 41-42.

Joseph Smith, in the Book of Moses, includes spirits, angels, men, and gods in this family.[5] He identifies Jesus and Satan as spirit brothers in the preexistent state. One of them, Jesus, received a body; the other, Satan, remained unembodied.

Because Brigham Young, a fanatical follower of Smith, inherited Smith's mantle, even today, Mormons dare not deny his authority as the prophet who succeeded Joseph Smith. Brigham Young assumed the presidency of the church when Joseph Smith and his brother Hyrum were lynched at the Carthage jail. His rivals for the office were pushed aside. The erratic Sidney Rigdon, who had been Smith's theologian from the earliest days, was voted out of office and left the church. David Whitmer, one of the celebrated "three witnesses," had already been excommunicated. James Strang and Alpheus Cutler both claimed to have had visions, which they insisted were indications that they were to succeed the prophet. All of these were outvoted, and each started his own branch of the church.

Brigham Young and his associates immediately took charge of the affairs of the church. Things were in hopeless chaos in Nauvoo, and Brigham started to effect plans for the church to go west to Utah, where they could be away from the influence of the United States. Utah was then under Spain.

Young was a competent leader and executive, but he was no theologian or scholar. By his own admission, he had attended school only eleven and a half

---

5. Joseph Smith, *Pearl of Great Price*, Book of Moses, chaps. 3-4.

days in his life.[6] In matters of religion, he was totally ignorant. By his own admission, he had rejected the idea of a conversion experience necessarily preceding baptism and admission to the church. He submitted to baptism in order to escape the harassment of those who were attempting to convert him.[7]

Smith's book and religious claims to be a prophet suited Young. He was the typical follower of a prophet. He did not have enough spiritual discernment to know if *The Book of Mormon* was true or false, but he liked Smith's philosophies. He accepted *The Book of Mormon*, converted, was baptized in his own millpond, and was made an elder "before his clothes were dry, the same day."[8]

At Smith's death, Young inherited the functions of "seer and prophet" as part of his office as president of the church. This gave him the prerogative of receiving revelations. This role was an unfamiliar one to Young. His directions were not from heaven through revelations, but from his own innate skill at leadership. His hunches were usually better than Smith's revelations.

Young adopted Smith's writings as sacred scripture and expounded them forcefully, loudly, and ungrammatically. He assumed the roles of pontiff in religious matters and dictator in political and financial affairs. His religion and politics were blended. Although he wrote little, most of his speeches were preserved in the *Journal of Discourses*, an official journal of the church. He preluded his messages

6. Morris Robert Werner, *Brigham Young*, p. 4.
7. Ibid., p. 9.
8. Ibid., p. 13.

with a command of authority in the manner of the Old
Testament prophets. Joseph Smith had done this as he
wrote his revelations, insisting that it was indeed the
Lord who was speaking.

On April 9, 1852, Brigham Young proclaimed the
Adam-God doctrine precisely.

> Now hear it, O inhabitants of the earth, Jew and
> Gentile, saint and sinner. When our father Adam
> came into the Garden of Eden, he came into it with a
> cellestial body, and brought Eve, one of his wives,
> with him. He helped to make and organize this world.
> He is Michael, the Archangel, the Ancient of Days
> about whom holy men have spoken—He is our Father
> and our God, and the only God with whom we have to
> do. Every man upon the earth, professing Christian or
> non-professing, must hear it, and will know it sooner
> or later . . . the earth was organized by three distinct
> characters, namely Elohim, Jehovah and Michael,
> these three forming a quorum, as in all heavenly
> bodies, and in organizing element, perfectly repre-
> sented in the Deity as Father, Son and Holy Ghost.[9]

Many Mormons today, when faced with this statement of Brigham Young's, will insist that we are mis-
quoting or misinterpreting what Young was trying to
teach. Apparently, however, his hearers accepted
what he said as truth, because in the following year
the doctrine was repeated in solid print in the
church's publication, *Millennial Star*, under the
heading, "Adam the Father and God of the human
family." The article says,

> The above sentiment appeared in *Star No. 48*, a

---

9. Brigham Young, in *Journal of Discourses* 1:50-51.

little to the surprise of some of its readers; and while
the statement may have appeared blasphemous to the
ignorant, it has no doubt given rise to some serious
reflections with the more candid and comprehensive
mind. . . . Adam is really God! And why not?[10]

A fuller statement on the same theme appears in a
later volume of the *Star*:

It has been said that Adam is the God and Father of
the human family, and persons are perhaps in fear
and great trouble of mind, lest they have to acknowledge him as such in a future day. For our part we
would rather acknowledge Adam to be our Father,
than hunt for another, and take up with the Devil.[11]

The development of the Adam-God doctrine of
Joseph Smith and Brigham Young was not accidental,
nor can it be attributed to these men's ignorance of the
Bible text. It was a deliberate departure from orthodoxy that paralleled other such departures. By
means of it, Mormons are able to bypass the complete
lordship of Jesus Christ and to substitute the lordship
of Adam as the God and Father of this world's system.
Instead of accepting the fact that the eternal God became incarnate in the person of Jesus Christ, and in
Him alone, Adam is made to be the incarnation of a
god who is "related" to man. Thus Adam, fallen and
restored, takes precedence over Jesus Christ.

Brigham Young stated that Adam became the actual father of the historic person Jesus of Nazareth,
and rejected the clearly stated biblical doctrine that
Mary was overshadowed by the Holy Ghost.

10. *Millennial Star* 15:801.
11. Ibid., 17:195.

As a final, blasphemous transfer to the prince of this world of the honor demanded by the Lord Jesus, the *Star* says,

> Every knee shall bow, and every tongue confess that he (Adam) is the God of the whole earth. Then will the words of the Prophet Brigham, when speaking of Adam, be fully realized—He is our Father and our God, and the only God with whom we have to do.[12]

Most of the church members accepted Young's dictum, because Young said it. One expressed the acceptance for all when he wrote: "I believe in the principle of obedience; and if I am told that Adam is our Father and our God, I just believe it."

Mormons who today deny that Smith and Young ever taught the doctrine must face the fact that it is still taught every day in the temples, at least by implication, in the endowment rituals where the creation scene is reenacted.[13]

In the temple ritual, Elohim, Jehovah, and Michael, impersonated by three Mormon priests, are presented as a triad of gods who, in consultation, view unorganized matter and propose to "Go down and organize it into a world like unto other worlds that have been hitherto organized."

The dialogue proceeds:

> JEHOVAH: We will go down.
> MICHAEL: We will go down.
> JEHOVAH: Michael, see, here is matter unorganized, we will organize it into a world like unto the other worlds that we have hithertofore formed, we

---

12. Ibid., 16:530.
13. Jerald and Sandra Tanner, *Mormonism, Shadow or Reality*, p. 466.

will call our labors the First Day and return and report.

MICHAEL: We will return and report our labors of
the First Day, Jehovah.

The same ritual is continued through the days of
creation until the sixth day. On the sixth day, one of
the three gods, Michael, is put to sleep and awakens
as Adam. Here is the ritual:

ELOHIM: Jehovah, see, the earth which we have
formed, there is no man to till and take care of it. We
will form man in our own likeness and image.

JEHOVAH: We will do so, Elohim.

ELOHIM: Brethren and Sisters, this is Michael, who
helped form the earth. When he awakes from the sleep
which we have caused to come upon him he will be
known as Adam and having forgotten everything,
will become as a little child.

Adam, awake!

Jehovah, is it good for man to be alone?

JEHOVAH: It is not good for man to be alone,
Elohim.

ELOHIM: We will make a deep sleep to come upon
this man whom we have formed and make for him a
woman to be a companion and helpmeet for him.

Brethren, close your eyes as if you were asleep.
Adam, awake and arise. All the brethren will please
arise. Adam, see the woman which we have formed to
be a companion and an helpmeet for you. What will
you call her?

ADAM: Eve.

ELOHIM: Why will you call her Eve?

ADAM: Because she is the Mother of all living.

ELOHIM: That is right, Adam. She is the Mother of
all living.

We will plant a garden eastward in Eden, and there we will put the man whom we have formed. Jehovah, introduce Adam into the Garden.

The ritual makes several things quite evident: (1) Jehovah and Elohim are made to be separate beings; (2) Michael is made to be a god; (3) Michael is made incarnate in the person of Adam; (4) thus, Adam is a god incarnate.

As for Joseph Fielding Smith's objection that Brigham Young is being misquoted or not understood, we say, in defense of Brigham, that he did not mean that Adam was the only god or the first god, but that he was the specific god assigned to this world, and therefore the only god with whom *we* have to do.

7

The Mormons and Jesus Christ

"What think ye of Christ?" (Matthew 22:42) is still the supreme test of orthodox Christianity. The Lord accepted Peter's confession, "Thou art the Christ, the Son of the living God," and on the basis of this confession, the structure of the Church is built (Matthew 16:15-18).

John's gospel introduces Jesus as the "Word of God," who was coequal and coeternal with the Father and the Spirit, and as the One by whom everything was created (John 1:3). John thus declares the eternal deity of our Lord. This same gospel introduces the fact of the incarnation as the step by which Deity assumed a veil of human flesh in order that He might reveal the Godhead in terms that man could understand. Having done this, He offered Himself as the only Substitute for the redemption of lost men that would be acceptable in God's sight (Hebrews 10:5-12).

Jesus Himself claimed to be Deity. Speaking to the Jews in the Temple, He claimed to be the eternal One who was before Abraham. He said, "Before Abraham

was, I am" (Gr., *ego eimi;* John 8:58). In using this
form of the verb "to be," He identified Himself with
the One who revealed Himself to Moses as the self-
existent One. This One instructed Moses, when He
appeared to him in the burning bush, to tell Israel, "I
AM hath sent me unto you" (Exodus 3:14). Thus the
One who spoke to the Jews at the Feast of Tabernacles
was the same One who spoke to Moses and identified
Himself as the eternal One, that is, Jehovah.

In the upper-room discourse, He identified Himself
as being One with the Father: "He that hath seen me
hath seen the Father" (John 14:9). In His great high-
priestly prayer, He claimed preexistence and coequal-
ity with the Father when He said, "Glorify thou me . . .
with the glory which I had with thee before the world
was" (John 17:5).

John, in stating the reason for writing his gospel,
said, "These [things] are written, that ye might believe that Jesus is the Christ, the Son of God; and that
believing ye might have life through his name"
(20:31).

Concerning His manhood, the Word declares that
He was begotten by the Holy Ghost of a virgin mother
(Matthew 1:20-21; Luke 1:35). The Word teaches His
impeccability. We read that He "did no sin" (1 Peter
2:22); He "knew no sin" (2 Corinthians 5:21); and "in
him is no sin" (1 John 3:5).

The Word teaches us that His death was voluntary.
Jesus said, "I lay down my life, that I might take it
again. No man taketh it from me, but I lay it down of
myself. I have power to lay it down, and I have power
to take it again" (John 10:17-18).

The Word teaches that Jesus was raised from the

dead without seeing corruption (Acts 2:27; 13:35-37). It teaches that He was raised from the dead physically. It teaches that His resurrection is the evidence of the validity of His work of redemption and that only through His resurrection is salvation from the penalty of sin assured to us (1 Corinthians 15:12-14).

In each of these propositions, Jesus Christ is unique. Each of these truths is vital and central to the teachings of orthodox Christianity.

The Mormons, in one way or another, deny all of these propositions. They deny that the Word who became flesh was unique in His eternality and co-equality with God; instead, they make Him merely one of the spirits of men, gods, and demons that, they claim, existed coequally with God.

The following statements suffice to state the Mormon position.

> Man is a spirit clothed with a tabernacle the intelligent part of which was never created or made but existed eternally—man was also in the beginning with God.[1]

> He (man) existed before he came to earth: He was with God "in the beginning." Man's destiny is divine. Man is an eternal being. He also is "from everlasting to everlasting."[2]

> Jesus Christ is not the father of the spirits who have taken or will take bodies, for He is one of them. He is the son and they are the sons and daughters of Elohim.[3]

> We have a succession of gods from Adam down to

---

1. Joseph Fielding Smith, *Progress of Man*, pp. 9-14.
2. John A. Widtsoe, *Varieties of American Religion*, p. 132.
3. James E. Talmage, *Articles of Faith*, p. 473.

Christ (his son) and his apostles at least all men, including Jesus Christ, being in the image of his father, and possessing a similar knowledge of good and evil.[4]

If I can pass Brother Joseph, I shall stand a good chance for passing Peter, Jesus and the prophets.[5]

As for the Devil and his fellow spirits, they are brothers to man and also to Jesus and sons and daughters of God in the same sense that we are.[6]

There is no impropriety . . . in speaking of Jesus Christ as the Elder Brother of the rest of human kind.[7]

The Mormons teach that Jesus was the natural born child of Adam and Mary.

When the Virgin Mary conceived the child Jesus . . . he was not begotten by the Holy Ghost. And who is his Father? He is the first of the human family.[8]

Jesus our elder brother, was begotten in the flesh by the same character that was in the garden of Eden.[9]

The Mormons believe that Jesus was not unique in His birth, boyhood, or manhood.

Jesus Christ, a little babe like all the rest of us, grew to be a man, was filled with a divine substance or fluid, called the Holy Spirit, by which he comprehended and spake the truth.[10]

The Mormons see no more in the life of Jesus than in

4. Richard, in *Millennial Star* 17:195-96.
5. Brigham Young, in *Journal of Discourses* 4:271.
6. John Henry Evans, *An American Prophet*, p. 241.
7. James E. Talmage, *Articles of Faith*, p. 472.
8. Young, in *Journal of Discourses* 1:50-51.
9. Ibid.
10. Parley P. Pratt, *Key to the Science of Theology*, p. 30.

any of us. Elder B. H. Roberts, in a footnote to Joseph Smith's *King Follett Discourse*, and quoting Sir Oliver Lodge as an authority on the subject, states,

> His humanity is to be recognized as real and ordinary—whatever happened to him may happen to any one of us.
>
> The divinity of Jesus, and the divinity of all other noble and stately souls, in so far as they, too, have been influenced by a spark of Deity—can be recognized as manifestations of the Divine."[11]

The Mormons see no uniqueness in the resurrection of Jesus Christ except in the fact that His resurrection preceded others. It has nothing to do with our salvation or justification. In *Key to the Science of Theology*, Pratt says,

> Every man who is eventually made perfect, raised from the dead, and filled or quickened with a fullness of celestial glory, will become like them (the Father and the Son) in every respect, physically and in intellect, attributes and powers.[12]

The Mormons teach that man is not saved by the redemptive work of Christ or through the shedding of His blood on Calvary. They believe, rather,

> The very germs of these Godlike attributes (of the Father and Son) being engendered in man, the offspring of Deity, only need cultivating, improving, developing and advancing by means of a series of changes, in order to arrive at the fountain head, the standard, the climax of Divine Humanity.[13]

11. B. H. Roberts, in Joseph Smith, *King Follett Discourse*, p. 11n.
12. Parley P. Pratt, p. 32.
13. Ibid., p. 32.

The Mormons believe that Jesus Christ was a polygamist. This is inescapable. The whole system of Mormon progress in life to come is based on the sealing of marriages in this life. Unmarried people and couples whose marriages are not sealed by the temple endowments become angels. Those sealed for eternity become gods.[14]

Jesus Christ, whom the Mormons admit to be a god, is considered to have been no more divine before His incarnation than any of us.[15] Thus, according to Mormon logic, if Jesus was not married during His earthly life, He could rise no higher than an angel in the next life.

The Mormons insist that Jesus was married at Cana of Galilee. Orson Hyde says,

> If at the marriage of Cana of Galilee, Jesus was the bridegroom and took unto him Mary, Martha and the other Mary, it shocks not our nerves. If there was not attachment and familiarity between our Saviour and these women, highly proper only in the relation of husband and wife, then we have no sense of propriety.[16]

Later, speaking on this same theme, Hyde says,

> If he never married, his intimacy with Mary and Martha, and the other Mary also, whom Jesus loved, must have been highly unbecoming and improper to say the best of it.[17]

The Mormons teach that Jesus had children before

14. Joseph Smith, *Doctrine and Covenants*, sec. 132.
15. Evans, p, 241.
16. Orson Hyde, in *Journal of Discourses* 2:81-82.
17. Ibid., 4:259.

His crucifixion. This, of course, follows in the Mormon line of reasoning; otherwise Jesus could not have complete exaltation in the next life. On this point, Hyde teaches,

> Did he multiply, and did he see his seed? Did he know his Father's law by complying with it, or did he not? Others may do as they like, but I will not charge our Saviour with neglect or transgression in this or any other duty.[18]

He continues in another sermon,

> We say it was Jesus Christ who was married whereby He could see His seed before He was crucified. I shall say here that before the Saviour died He looked upon His own natural children as we look upon ours. When Mary came to the sepulchre she saw two angels and she said unto them "they have taken away my Lord or husband."[19]

The Mormons use the name of Jesus Christ in the title of their church, but any discerning Christian will readily observe that this is not the Jesus Christ whom we worship as the eternal Son of God who died for our sins according to the Scriptures. Theirs is not the Christ of whom Peter said,

> Neither is there salvation in any other: for there is none other name under heaven given among men, whereby we must be saved (Acts 4:12).

Neither is theirs the Saviour of whom Paul said:

> Who was delivered for our offenses, and was

18. Ibid.
19. Ibid., 4:210.

raised again for our justification. Therefore being justified by faith, we have peace with God through our
Lord Jesus Christ (Romans 4:25—5:1).

Mormon theology does not accept or comprehend
the Christian doctrine of the incarnation. Mormons
believe, of course, that there was a historic character
named Jesus of Nazareth and will accept the fact that
He was born miraculously to a person named Mary.
(Muslims also would agree to this.) They call Him
"the Christ" and, in a vague way, accord to Him the
status of a savior. However, because of their peculiar
doctrines of polytheism, the preexistence of human
spirits, and the ability of men to become gods, they
cannot consider Jesus to be the unique and only begotten Son, who, as the eternal Word, was one with
God from eternity.

Joseph Smith taught that man was in the beginning
with God. John 1:1-4 explicitly states,

> In the beginning was the Word, and the Word was
> with God, and the Word was God. The same was in the
> beginning with God. All things were made by him;
> and without him was not any thing made that was
> made. In him was life; and the life was the light of
> men.

The title page of Joseph Smith's blasphemous *Inspired Version* reads: *The Holy Scriptures: Translated and Corrected by the Spirit of Revelation.* It was
completed by July, 1833. In it, Smith gives the following reading of the early verses of John's gospel:

> In the beginning was the gospel preached through
> the Son. And the gospel was the word, and the word
> was with the Son, and the Son was with God, and the

> Son was of God. The same was in the beginning with
> God. All things were made by him; and without him
> was not anything made which was made. In him was
> the gospel, and the gospel was the life, and the life
> was the light of men.[20]

This is not honest or even well-intentioned para-
phrasing of the text of Scripture but is a poorly dis-
guised attempt on Smith's part to create Scripture that
would divest the Son of His eternality as one with the
Father. The term *the Word (logos)* is obviously a name
of God the Son, and not, as Smith has it, an abstract
equation with the Gospel.

The crude Mormon doctrine held by Joseph Smith
and Brigham Young is in sharp contrast to the Christian doctrine that the Word is the eternal Son. Parley
P. Pratt, one of the first Mormon "twelve," expressed
the doctrine as, "Gods, angels and men, are all of one
species, one race, one great family, widely diffused
among the planetary systems as colonies, kingdoms,
nations, etc."[21]

Joseph Smith indicates his belief that Satan and
Jesus were spirit brothers and sons of God before the
spirit of Jesus was given a body by Mary in
Bethlehem. In his Book of Moses, where he has Satan
and Jesus contending for the privilege of taking a
body of flesh so as to become the redeemer, Jesus wins
the contest.[22]

Brigham Young complicates the problem with his
Adam-God doctrine, in which he makes Michael, the
archangel whom Smith equates with the "Ancient of

---

20. Joseph Smith, Inspired Version, John 1:1-4.
21. Parley P. Pratt, p. 30.
22. Joseph Smith, *Pearl of Great Price*, Book of Moses 4:1-4.

Days," become incarnate in Adam. He then makes Adam, resurrected and glorified, the father of Jesus. He rejects the biblical account of the conception of Jesus in the womb of Mary, insisting that Jesus was not begotten by the Holy Spirit. He says,

> When the Virgin Mary conceived the child Jesus, the father had begotten him in his own likeness. He was not begotten by the Holy Ghost. And who is the Father? He is the first of the human family.[23]

Hosea Stout, a contemporary of Young and a prominent Mormon, writes, "Another meeting this evening. President B. Young taught that Adam was the father of Jesus and the only God to us, that he came to this world in a resurrected body."[24]

In a conversation between Abraham H. Cannon and his father, George Q. Cannon, it is assured that the doctrine continued to be held after the death of Brigham Young. The conversation was held in 1888. Abraham Cannon writes,

> Father . . . asked me what I understood concerning Mary conceiving the Savior: and I found no answer. He asked me what was to prevent Father Adam from visiting and overshadowing the mother of Jesus. "Then," said I, "He must have been a resurrected being." "Yes," he said, "and though Christ is said to have been the firstfruits of them that slept, yet the Savior said he did nothing but what he had seen his Father do, for He had power to lay down His life and take it up again. Adam, though made of dust, was

23. Young, in *Journal of Discourses* 1:50-51.
24. Hosea Stout, *On the Mormon Frontier: The Diary of Hosea Stout* 2:435.

made, as president Young said, of the dust of another planet than this."[25]

An element in the church has tried to obscure the Adam-God doctrine and Adam as the father of Jesus. This is not because it is not believed but because it is not popular.

Whether by accident or by design, Brigham Young and Joseph Smith's doctrine of Adam-God eliminates the doctrine of the uniqueness of the birth of Jesus Christ, born of a virgin and begotten by the Holy Ghost. It bypasses the significance of the incarnation by making it one of a series of such incarnations and by making the virgin birth of Jesus Christ secondary to the incarnation of the Ancient of Days as a human figure, Adam. Thus, Adam has precedence over Jesus.

---

25. Abraham H. Cannon, *Daily Journal of Abraham H. Cannon*, 10:178-79.

8

The Mormons
and the Holy Spirit

There is no phase of Christian doctrine that demands more careful and discerning study than the subject of the person and work of the Holy Spirit.

For the purpose of establishing a definitive standard by which to evaluate the Mormon concept of this doctrine, we submit the following outline, which, we believe, will satisfy all truly orthodox Christians.

I. The Holy Spirit is identified in Scripture as having a distinct personality and is not merely an influence.
   A. He is referred to in the third person, masculine gender, singular: He, Him, His (John 14:17, 26; 16:13).
   B. Ananias lied to the Holy Spirit (Acts 5:3-4). One cannot lie to an influence.
   C. The Holy Spirit gave instruction for the ordination of Paul and Barnabas (Acts 13:2). An influence could not do this.
II. The Holy Spirit is identified in His relationship to the Trinity as being coequal and coeternal with the Father and the Son (Genesis 1:26; 11:7;

Isaiah 6:8; 48:13-16; Matthew 3:16; 28:19; John 15:26; 2 Corinthians 13:14; Ephesians 2:18; Hebrews 9:14).

III. The Holy Spirit is identified as having the attributes of Deity.
  A. Eternality—Hebrews 9:14.
  B. Omnipotence—Psalm 104:30.
  C. Omnipresence—Psalm 139:7.
  D. Omniscience—Isaiah 40:13; 1 Corinthians 2:10-11.

IV. The Holy Spirit performs special tasks.
  A. He is the Author of the Word of God (2 Timothy 3:16; 2 Peter 1:21).
  B. He is the "Architect" of the universe (Genesis 1:2, 26; Job 26:13; Psalm 104:30).
  C. He is the Agent of the Trinity who deals with man.
    1. In Genesis 6:3, He strives with man.
    2. In Job 32:8, He gives understanding.
    3. In Exodus 31:2-5, He imparts skill.
    4. In Judges 14:6, He gives physical vigor.
    5. In Numbers 11:25; Judges 11:29; 2 Samuel 23:2; 2 Peter 1:21, He empowers the servants of God.
  D. The Holy Spirit is the Agent of the new birth.
    1. In John 16:7-11, He convicts and enlightens concerning sin, righteousness, and judgment.
    2. In John 3:5-6, He regenerates.
    3. In Ephesians 1:13-14, He seals the believers.
    4. In 1 Corinthians 12:13, He baptizes the believers into one Body, the Church.

   E. The Holy Spirit activates and empowers be-
      lievers, as individuals and collectively as the
      Church.
      1. In John 14:17; Romans 8:9-11, He in-
         dwells.
      2. In John 14:26; 16:13; 1 John 2:27, He in-
         structs.
      3. In Romans 8:26-27, He intercedes between
         man and the Father.
      4. In Romans 8:4 and 2 Corinthians 5:7, He
         empowers the believer to walk the walk of
         faith.
   F. The Holy Spirit is the Custodian of the
      Church while on this earth (John 14:16; 2
      Thessalonians 2:16-17) and involved in her
      call home as the Body of Christ (Revelation
      22:17).

One could go on endlessly outlining the various
aspects of the person and work of the Holy Spirit, but
this should suffice for purposes of comparison between Christian and Mormon concepts.

Now let us examine the Mormon attitude.

The first item of the Mormon doctrinal statement
simply states: "We believe in God the Eternal Father,
and in His Son Jesus Christ and in the Holy Ghost."[1]
This could mean anything. In *Doctrine and Covenants*, we read, "The Father has a body of flesh and
bones as tangible as man's; the Son also; but the Holy
Ghost has not a body of flesh and bones, but is a
personage of Spirit."[2]

Some of the Mormon expositors have variable con-

1. Joseph Smith, *Pearl of Great Price*, Articles of Faith, p. 60.
2. Joseph Smith, *Doctrine and Covenants*, 130:22.

victions concerning the identity of the person of the Holy Spirit. Orson Pratt remarks:

> I am inclined to think, from some things in the revelations, that there is such a personal being as a personal Holy Ghost, but it is not set forth as a positive fact, and the Lord has never given me any revelation upon the subject and consequently I cannot make up my mind one way or the other.[3]

From the beginning, Mormon theologians have had problems trying to distinguish between the Holy Ghost and the Holy Spirit, whom they indicate are separate entities. One, the Holy Ghost, is a personage of spirit and, as Joseph Fielding Smith indicates, is the mind of the Father and the Son.[4] The following excerpts are from Smith's chapter on the Holy Ghost.

> The Holy Spirit, or Spirit of God, both of which terms are sometimes used interchangeably with the Holy Ghost, is the influence of Deity, the light of Christ, or of truth, which proceeds from the presence of God to fill the immensity of space, and to quicken the understanding of man. . . . The Holy Ghost as a personage of Spirit can no more be omnipresent in person than can the Father or the Son, but by his intelligence, his knowledge, his power and influence, over and through the laws of nature, he is and can be omnipresent throughout all the works of God. . . . You may call it the Spirit of God, you may call it the influence of God's intelligence, you may call it the substance of his power, no matter what it is called, it is the spirit of intelligence that permeates the universe and gives to the spirits of men understanding.

3. Orson Pratt, in *Journal of Discourses* 2:338.
4. Joseph Fielding Smith, *Gospel Doctrine*, pp. 67-68.

> . . . The Spirit of God which emanates from Deity may
> be likened to electricity, or the universal ether . . .
> which fills the earth and the air, and is everywhere
> present.[5]

Mormon teachers usually refer to the Holy Spirit as
"it," as may be noted in the previous quotation. Parley
Pratt, brother of Orson who was quoted above, expresses the subject in a fashion that reflects the thinking of most Mormons. He says,

> This substance, like all others, is one of the ele-
> ments of material, or physical existence, and there-
> fore subject to the necessary laws which govern all
> matter. Like all other matters, its whole is composed
> of individual particles. Like them, each particle oc-
> cupies space, possesses the power of motion, requires
> time to move from one place to another, and can in no
> wise occupy two spaces at once. In these respects it
> differs nothing from all other matter. It penetrates the
> pores of the most solid substances, pierces the human
> system to its most inward recesses, discerns the
> thoughts and intents of the heart. It has power to move
> through space with inconceivable velocity, far ex-
> ceeding the tardy motions of electricity or of physical
> light. It comprehends the past, present and future in
> all their fullness. It is endowed with knowledge, wis-
> dom, truth, love, charity, justice, and mercy in all
> their ramifications.[6]

Mormons deny that the Lord Jesus was conceived
in the womb of the virgin Mary by the Holy Spirit.
Joseph Smith laid the groundwork for the doctrine by
establishing Adam as a deity.[7]

---

5. Ibid., pp. 60-61.
6. Parley P. Pratt, *Key to the Science of Theology,* pp. 39-40.
7. Joseph Smith, *Doctrine and Covenants,* 27:11; 78: 16; 116:1;
   197:54.

Brigham Young followed logically by declaring,

> When the Virgin Mary conceived the child Jesus, the Father had begotten him in his own likeness. He was not begotten by the Holy Ghost, and who is his father? He is the first of the human family—now remember from this time forth, and forever, that Jesus Christ was not begotten by the Holy Ghost.[8]

What a contrast between the blasphemous views of the Mormons and the crystal-clear statements of Scripture! Matthew's gospel says,

> The angel of the Lord appeared unto him in a dream, saying . . . fear not to take unto thee Mary thy wife: for that which is conceived in her is of the Holy Ghost (1:20).

Luke's gospel records,

> And the angel answered and said unto her, The Holy Ghost shall come upon thee, and the power of the Highest shall overshadow thee: therefore also that holy thing which shall be born of thee shall be called the Son of God (1:35).

The failure of Mormons to understand the true nature of the Holy Spirit—as a person and yet totally nonphysical—is a result of their concept of the godhead as being composed of separate physical persons. They reason that if God, the Father, and Jesus Christ, His Son, are separate "personages of flesh and bones," how can a Person of the Godhead be pure spirit and still be a person? Thus, in their thinking, the Spirit must be an element dispensed in varying quantities to each individual. They cannot accept the

---

8. Brigham Young, in *Journal of Discourses* 1:50-51.

Christian doctrine of the Spirit of God indwelling believers subsequent to the new birth and thereby indwelling the Body of Christ, the Church. They cannot conceive of the Holy Spirit as being universally resident in believers. They say: "How can a personal Holy Spirit be indwelling separate people at the same time?"[9] This same sort of reasoning is responsible for their concept of God the Father as being not purely "spirit." Joseph Fielding Smith, in commenting on Jesus' statement to the woman of Sychar that "God is a Spirit" (John 4:24), says, "This I do not believe."[10]

James L. Barker, in *The Divine Church*, with this same limited concept, says, " 'No man hath seen God at any time' [John 1:18] is not in harmony with other scriptures." He reasons that "in such cases, either the text has not come down correctly to the present or it has been incorrectly translated."[11]

The reason Mormon thought cannot comprehend the oneness of the Trinity and at the same time the personality of the Spirit is because of their failure to recognize that all divine propositions cannot be confined within the limits of human expression.

In *The Pearl of Great Price*, Joseph Smith implies that since God spoke "face to face" with Moses, Moses was looking at a physical personage with physical eyes. The phrase "face to face" is the Hebrew expression conveying intimacy. The Bible is full of such anthropomorphisms. They do not imply that God is corporeal but indicate that He communicated Himself in expressions familiar to men. Thus Joseph Smith

9. Orson Pratt, *Absurdities of Materialism*, p. 24.
10. Joseph Fielding Smith, *Teachings of Joseph Smith*, p. 85.
11. James L. Barker, *The Divine Church*, p. 9.

had to reject the later statement in Exodus (33:20), "Thou canst not see my face . . . and live," as a contradiction to the earlier statement, "The LORD spake unto Moses face to face" (33:11). The only difficulty here is the limitation of human language—or rather, in Smith's inability to understand the significance of scriptural language and values.

Joseph Smith and most Mormons insist on interpreting given portions of Scripture within the limitations of the English of the King James Version of the Bible.

It is quite evident from this discussion of Deity that the Christian doctrine of the Trinity cannot be accepted by Mormons. To them, gods must be exalted humans, and the Holy Ghost has not received a body; therefore, He cannot be a god.

Their concept that the Father is greater than the Son limits the Son's status in the Mormon trinity.

The Mormons are not bothered by the mathematical problem of the Christian Trinity. Rather, they do not believe that the Persons of the godhead are coequal and coeternal. If they believed in this great central truth, they would have to believe in the lordship of Jesus Christ.

9

The Mormon Doctrine of Man

Satan aspired to be "like the most High" (Isaiah 14:14). In his rebellion, he lost his previous status and was cast out of heaven. Man was not created to be an angel or a servant, as was Lucifer, but to have rule over the earth and to have fellowship with God. Satan, in his revenge, sought to destroy God's new creature, man, and approached the human pair in Eden with the same strategy as he had used in his rebellion against the Most High—a strategy that had cost him his position.

Satan told the woman, "Ye shall be as gods, knowing good and evil" (Genesis 3:5). The woman ate of the forbidden fruit and gave of it to Adam. They came to know the great facts of good and evil experimentally. But they had fallen, for they had disobeyed the specific command of God. Mormons erroneously teach that the Fall was a physical change in body structure as the result of the malign effects of a piece of fruit.

A few thousands of years later, Joseph Smith took the words out of Satan's mouth and propounded a new doctrine: that men may become gods. The Mormons promise deity to all the faithful. Joseph Smith stated the proposition thus: "You have got to learn how to be Gods yourselves—the same as all the Gods have done before you."[1]

In order to elevate man to the status of deity, it was necessary for Smith to lower the stature of his god. He does this by stating, "God . . . was once a man like us!"[2] Given this latitude, the Mormon theologians enlarged on the idea and developed their present concept of man as a potential god.

Lorenzo Snow, a contemporary of Joseph Smith, codified Smith's teaching in the following aphorism. It is now in standard usage with Mormon teachers.

> As man is, God was.
> As God is, man may become.[3]

Another contemporary of Smith, Orson Hyde, recognized by the Mormons as one of their greatest theologians, said,

> Remember that God our heavenly Father was perhaps once a child, and mortal like we are, and rose step by step in the scale of progress, in the school of advancement; has moved forward and overcome until he has arrived at the point where he now is.[4]

Having thus reduced the stature of Deity to that of an elevated superman, the Mormon teachers have had little trouble developing a "doctrine of man" that places man on a par with such a deity. Needless to say, the Mormon god is not the God of the Bible, nor is the Mormon man the creature who came from the hand of

---

1. Joseph Smith, *King Follett Discourse*, p. 10.
2. Ibid., p. 9.
3. Ibid., n.
4. Orson Hyde, in *Journal of Discourses* 1:123.

the Lord God by the process stated in Genesis 2:7: "And the LORD God formed man of the dust of the ground, and breathed into his nostrils the breath of life; and man became a living soul."

In order to develop such a God-man theory, it was necessary for the Mormons to develop their own particular doctrine of reincarnation. Not that the doctrine is new with them: they have merely changed some of the wording.* Their theories fit perfectly with the ancient mystery religions. Milton Hunter accepts these without hesitation.[5]

First, they teach that all human beings and spirits, and even Jesus Christ and Satan, existed as spirit beings from an eternity past. At physical birth, the spirits are given bodies in which they can exercise their choices of right and wrong. Thus the present life is a period of probation. The manner in which this probationary period is utilized determines completely the status of the individual in the life after the resurrection.

The afterlife starts where the present life ends. If the deeds and accomplishments in this life have been satisfactory and all temple endowments have been fulfilled, the individual becomes a god and is considered eligible to procreate spirit children and populate worlds of his own, as Adam and Eve did in this world. The process goes on, ad infinitum. No good Mormon will deny that this is standard Mormon doctrine. But,

---

* The reincarnation of Mormonism is not that of the Eastern religions, in which there is the possibility of regression to animal form if accomplishments do not suffice to assure reincarnation in a human body. It is the reincarnation of the old Babylonian mystery religions where a spirit becomes a human, and then at death becomes a god.

5. Milton R. Hunter, *The Gospel Through the Ages*, chap. 16.

lest someone question the accuracy of our statements, we will quote from standard and approved Mormon theologians.

Joseph Smith prepared the way for later Mormon teachers when he rewrote the creation story. He placed this material both in his Book of Moses (a section of *The Pearl of Great Price*) and in the *Inspired Version*. The Salt Lake Mormons use the former, while the Reorganized Church uses the latter.

> For I, the Lord God, created all things of which I have spoken, spiritually, before they were naturally upon the face of the earth ... for in heaven I created them ... and man became a living soul; the first flesh upon the earth, the first man also; nevertheless, all things were before created, but spiritually were they created and made, according to my word.[6]

In this same volume, Smith has the Lord saying to Enoch,

> Anoint thine eyes with clay, and wash them, and thou shalt see; and he did so. And he beheld the spirits that God had created, and he beheld also things which were not visible to the natural eye.[7]

A few months later, certainly not later than 1835, Joseph Smith had prepared the final chapters of *The Pearl of Great Price*. These he called the Book of Abraham and claimed to have translated them from papyri found on a mummy purchased from a traveling showman, Michael N. Chandler.[8]

There were four mummies in the collection. One of

---

6. Joseph Smith, *Inspired Version*, Genesis 2:5-9.
7. Ibid., Genesis 6:37-38.
8. Fawn M. Brodie, *No Man Knows My History: The Life of Joseph Smith, the Mormon Prophet*, p. 170.

these was ascertained by Smith to be that of Pharaoh's daughter (Fourteenth Dynasty), another was that of Pharaoh Necho (Twenty-sixth Dynasty). On the mummy of Pharaoh's daughter were papyri with Abraham's handwriting (Eleventh Dynasty). From these Eleventh Dynasty papyri, found in the wrapping of a Fourteenth Dynasty mummy purchased together with a Twenty-sixth Dynasty mummy, Joseph Smith translated his Book of Abraham.

To the credit of the Reorganized Church, when the hoax was exposed by competent Egyptologists, they repudiated the Book of Abraham. The balance of *The Pearl of Great Price* they must accept since it is the identical matter found in the *Inspired Version*. One wonders how they can reject Smith's hoax without rejecting Smith.

In this Book of Abraham, we read the following:

> Now the Lord had shown unto me, Abraham, the intelligences that were organized before the world was; and among all these there were many of the noble and great ones; and God saw these souls that were good, and he stood in the midst of them, and he said: These I will make my rulers; for he stood among those that were spirits, and he saw that they were good; and he said unto me: Abraham, thou art one of them; thou wast chosen before thou wast born. And there stood one among them that was like unto God, and he said unto those who were with him: We will go down, for there is space there, and we will take of these materials, and we will make an earth whereon these may dwell. . . . And the Lord said: Whom shall I send? And one answered like unto the Son of Man: Here am I, send me. And another answered and said: Here am I, send me. And the Lord said: I will send the

first. And the second was angry, and kept not his first
estate; and at that day, many followed after him.[9]

With this pseudobiblical background, the Mormon
theologians have gone to work in real earnest to develop the theory.

Students of Church history will recognize a similarity to the "precreated spirits" doctrine of Origen and
others. I doubt if Smith ever heard of Origen and his
heresies, although Rigdon may have been acquainted
with Origen's theory. Later teachers among Mormons
do use Origen's writings to confirm their teaching,
but I believe Smith reached his conclusions in the
same manner as Origen: by theorizing in an area in
which the Bible is silent. Commenting on such
theorizers, Lewis Sperry Chafer says,

> There is much room where God has not spoken for
> theologians to fill in large portions wholly agreeable
> to their way of thinking; then in later developments of
> their system, they draw out of their own creation
> precisely what they have prepared and need.[10]

This, precisely, was the practice of Smith and is the
practice of all the Mormon commentators. The following quotations indicate a few of the developments
of the doctrine by later Mormon writers.

> Jesus Christ is not the Father of the spirits who have
> taken or yet shall take bodies upon this earth, for He is
> one of them.[11]

> It is the belief of the Latter-day Saints that the earth
> was organized in order that personages of spirit—the

9. Joseph Smith, *Pearl of Great Price,* Book of Abraham 3:22-28.
10. Lewis Sperry Chafer, *Systematic Theology* 2:169.
11. James E. Talmage, *Articles of Faith,* pp. 472-73.

spiritual children of God—might have a place where
they could take upon themselves mortality—take
mortal bodies. It was necessary for them to become
mortal before they could learn good from evil, joy
from sorrow. It was necessary to become mortal in
order to have increase, children to learn the ways of
God and obey his laws.[12]

Joseph Fielding Smith, one of the staunchest of the
Utah Mormon theologians, said,

The Bible[†] teaches us that man existed in the spirit
creation before he appeared on this earth with his
physical body, but this doctrine in the Bible is only
discerned through a mist or fog. This fog is created, as
recorded by Nephi, because many plain and precious
things have been taken out of the Bible. . . . The
doctrine of man's pre-existence in the spirit creation
is clearly and forcefully taught.[13]

The Latter-Day Saints believe that man is a spirit
clothed with a tabernacle. The intelligent part of this
tabernacle was never created or made, but existed
eternally. This belief is based upon a revelation given
to the church on May 6, 1833, at Kirtland, Ohio.

Man was also in the beginning with God. Intelli-
gence, or the light of truth, was not created or made,
neither indeed can be. . . . For man is spirit. The
elements are eternal, and spirit and element, insepar-
ably connected, receive a fulness of joy.[14]

---

12. Bardella Shipp Curtis, *Sacred Scriptures and Religious Phi-
    losophy*, n.p.
 † Joseph Fielding Smith is referring to the Bible as rewritten by
    Joseph Smith and known as the *Inspired Version.*
13. Joseph Fielding Smith, *The Progress of Man*, pp. 9-10.
14. Joseph Smith, *Doctrine and Covenants*, 93:29, 33.

Joseph Fielding Smith, writing in a letter to Elder Whitney, says,

> Our knowledge of persons and things before we came here, combined with the divinity awakened within our souls through obedience to the gospel . . . guides our preferences in the course of this life. . . . Can we know anything here that we did not know before we came? . . . I believe that our saviour possessed a foreknowledge of all of the vicissitudes through which he would pass in the mortal tabernacle. If Christ knew beforehand, so did we. But in coming here we forget all, that our agency might be free indeed to choose good or evil.[15]

James E. Talmage, in explaining the transition from the previous state of man, states,

> It has been shown that mortality is divinely provided as a means of schooling and test, whereby the spirit offspring of God may develop their powers and demonstrate their characters. Every one of us has been advanced from the unembodied or pre-existent state to our present condition, in which the individual spirit is temporarily united with a body of flesh and bones.[16]

Later in this same chapter, Talmage refers to Jesus Christ as "the first born among all the spirit children of God," who "was to come to earth . . . to teach men the saving principles of the eternal Gospel."[17]

To Mormons, the Fall was a fortuitous episode—distressing, no doubt, at the time, but absolutely necessary for the final advancement of men.

---

15. Joseph Fielding Smith, *Gospel Doctrine*, pp. 15-16.
16. James E. Talmage, *The Vitality of Mormonism*, pp. 48-49.
17. Ibid.

Regarding the Fall, Talmage writes,

> Through partaking of food unsuited to their condi-
> tion and against which they had been specifically
> forewarned, the man and his wife became subject to
> physical degeneracy.[18]

Probably one of the most concise Mormon statements regarding man, his origin, and his destiny has
been made by John A. Widtsoe.

> He (man) existed before he came to earth; he was
> with God in the beginning; he accepted the opportu-
> nity provided by his father to come on earth to be
> tried, refined and educated; he lives on earth under
> laws and regulations and the authority of the Lord: he
> shall die, but in time he shall regain his body, and
> because of his righteous endeavors shall go on forever
> into eternal, active, progressive exaltation. Man's des-
> tiny is divine. Life on earth is but a chapter in an
> eternal journey. Man is an eternal being. He also is
> "from everlasting to everlasting."
>
> In this manner of thinking, salvation acquires a
> definite meaning. Whoever is in process of develop-
> ment or progression is in process of salvation. In-
> creasing knowledge, used in conformity with the
> plan of the Lord, becomes power to remove all obsta-
> cles to progress. In the words of Joseph Smith, to be
> saved is to be placed "beyond the power of evil."
>
> Clearly then, our salvation begun in the dim past, is
> being worked out by us on earth and will be ap-
> proached in its greater perfection throughout the end-
> less ages of future life. By this token all men may be
> saved but in degrees proportionate to their righteous
> works.

18. Ibid., pp. 49-50.

Does a man then save himself? From one point of view, yes. However, it is only through the divine plan that salvation may be won; therefore, man is only a partner in the saving process. Salvation is a co-operative enterprise between God and man.[19]

Contrast the complicated God-man theories with a simple statement of Scripture:

The LORD God formed man of the dust of the ground, and breathed into his nostrils the breath of life; and man became a living soul (Genesis 2:7).

Dr. Talmage's statement (on a previous page), that Adam and Eve partook of food that was unsuited to their condition and thus became mortal, needs some amplifying. As has been stated elsewhere, the Mormons teach that Adam (formerly Michael) and one of his wives came to this earth to help organize and populate it. Prior to their coming, they were celestial beings. In describing the arrival of Adam and Eve, and the Fall, Joseph Fielding Smith taught,

Man became a living spirit clothed with a physical, flesh and bones body, but the body was NOT quickened by blood, but by spirit, for THERE WAS NO BLOOD IN ADAM'S BODY BEFORE THE FALL. HE WAS NOT THEN "FLESH" AS WE KNOW IT, THAT IS IN THE SENSE OF MORTALITY.[20]

19. John A. Widtsoe, *Varieties of American Religion*, pp. 132-33.
20. Joseph Fielding Smith, *Doctrine of Salvation*, p. 92.

Follow the sequence: Adam came from a celestial world where he was a spiritual being; he received a flesh-and-bones body; he ate fruit that was unsuitable to his spiritual body; thus, he fell and became mortal; and not until then did his body contain blood. Yet before the Fall he walked and talked, breathed and ate, and had a surgical operation performed in which a rib was extracted and the wound healed.

The Mormons, of course, quote their own scriptures to prove their doctrine. The only biblical portions that they fall back on are the following:

1. Psalm 139:17-18, "Thine eyes did see my substance, yet being unperfect; and in thy book all my members were written . . . when as yet there was none of them." This, to anyone who understands English grammar, is a discussion of the omniscience of God and not the preexistence of man.

2. John 9:2, "Who did sin, this man, or his parents, that he was born blind?" They argue that this man must have had a previous experience or he could not have sinned before he was born. The problem is that they are ignorant of Jewish beliefs at the time of the Lord Jesus. The following quotation from Charles L. Feinberg, probably one of the most knowledgeable Jewish Christians today, should explain the passage.

> I am afraid that any doctrine of the pre-existence of man is quite unaware of the theological position of the Jews of our Lord's day. It is known from the literature of the Jews that the rabbis argued whether an individual could sin before birth. There was certainly no general agreement on this matter. Those who ask the question in John 9 were evidently among the

number who felt that a child could sin before birth.[21]

Obviously the whole unbiblical, illogical, and non-Christian concept of man's preexistence is contrived in Mormon doctrine to avoid the implication that man is a sinner by nature and by practice and must rely entirely on the redemptive work of Christ if he is to have the forgiveness of sins here and eternal life hereafter.

_____

21. Dr. Charles L. Feinberg to author, July 2, 1965.

10

The Priesthood

One of the distinctives of the Church of the Lord Jesus Christ since the day of Pentecost is of belief in the priesthood of all believers and in the Lord Jesus as our great High Priest. Hebrews 9 gives as conclusive a definition of the priesthood of the Lord Jesus as can be stated.

> Christ being come an high priest of good things to come, by a greater and more perfect tabernacle, not made of hands, that is to say, not of this building; neither by the blood of goats and calves, but by his own blood he entered in once into the holy place, having obtained eternal redemption for us. For if the blood of bulls and of goats, and the ashes of an heifer sprinkling the unclean, sanctifieth to the purifying of the flesh: how much more shall the blood of Christ, who through the eternal Spirit offered himself without spot to God, purge your conscience from dead works to serve the living God? (vv. 11-14).

The past, present, and future of the priesthood ministry of Jesus Christ in our behalf is given in verses 24-28.

> For Christ is not entered into the holy places made with hands, which are the figures of the true; but into

heaven itself, now to appear in the presence of God for us: nor yet that he should offer himself often, as the high priest entereth into the holy place every year with blood of others; for then must he often have suffered since the foundation of the world: but now once in the end of the world hath he appeared to put away sin by the sacrifice of himself. And as it is appointed unto men once to die, but after this the judgment: so Christ was once offered to bear the sins of many; and unto them that look for him shall he appear the second time without sin unto salvation.

Joseph Smith, in announcing the finding and translation of *The Book of Mormon*, declared that it was the book that told of a "new and everlasting covenant." He also declared that angels had communicated with him, assuring him that he would be the prophet of the restoration of the true church.

Today the Mormon church claims a priesthood that includes deacons in their teens and nonagenarian presidents. Boys hold the lesser, or Aaronic priesthood; elders are ordained to the Melchizedek priesthood at maturity and as they qualify. The names of the two priesthoods are the only element that lends a religious flavor to the structure of the priesthood. There is no similarity between the biblical rituals and priestly services of the Old Testament and the rituals of the Mormon church. The latter are more pagan than Christian or Jewish. The New Testament Church had no sacerdotal priesthood. It teaches the priesthood of all believers.

Besides providing an outlet for the religious expression of the Mormons, the priesthood exists as an organizational, administrative, and managerial struc-

ture for a unified, religio-societal, and commercial
quasi corporation of unbounded wealth. The fact that
the Mormons are a religion-based establishment gives
them vast tax-exempt privileges.

Mormon propagandists will almost invariably ask
Christian workers, "Where do you get your authority?" By this question they are implying that they
have authority to speak in religious matters and that
the religious denominations have no such authority,
since, as Joseph Smith claimed, the established
church of his day had lost its authority and had no
priests capable of administering the rites of the
church. The Mormon "authority" is based on the au-
thenticity of the priesthood, which goes back to a
claimed incident in the experience of Joseph Smith
and Oliver Cowdery as they were translating *The
Book of Mormon.* Here is the statement, taken from
Joseph Smith's own story as given in *The Pearl of
Great Price.*

> We still continued the work of translation, when, in
> the ensuing month (May, 1829) we on a certain day
> went into the woods to pray and inquire of the Lord
> respecting baptism for the remissions of sins, that we
> found mentioned in the translation of the plates.
> While we were thus employed, praying and calling
> upon the Lord, a messenger from heaven descended
> in a cloud of light, and having laid his hands upon us,
> he ordained us, saying:
>   *Upon you my fellow servants, in the name of Mes-
> siah, I confer the Priesthood of Aaron, which holds
> the keys of the ministering of angels, and of the gospel
> of repentance, and of baptism by immersion for the
> remission of sins; and this shall never be taken again*

> *from the earth until the sons of Levi do offer again an offering unto the Lord in righteousness.*
>
> He said this Aaron Priesthood had not the power of laying on of hands for the gift of the Holy Ghost, but that this should be conferred on us hereafter; and he commanded us to go and be baptized, and gave us directions that I should baptize Oliver Cowdery, and that afterwards he should baptize me.
>
> Accordingly we went and were baptized. I baptized him first, and afterwards he baptized me—after which I laid my hands upon his head and ordained him to the Aaronic Priesthood, and afterwards he laid his hands on me and ordained me to the same Priesthood—for so we were commanded.[1]

What is wrong with this picture? Practically everything. Smith says that it was the angel John the Baptist that appeared to himself and Cowdery, ordained them to the Aaronic priesthood, and promised that later they would be ordained to the Melchizedek priesthood.

John the Baptist is not an angel, never was an angel, nor will he ever be an angel. John was a very physical man who appeared at a point in history, fulfilled his mission, was beheaded at the whim of a lustful woman, and was buried. He is still in the grave and will be there until the resurrection, when he will get his head back.

John the Baptist, while a descendant of Aaron and therefore eligible to the priesthood, was not a priest and did not administer any priestly rites. He could have succeeded to the office of his father, Zacharias, who was a priest in the order of Abia, but that was not

---

1. Joseph Smith, *Pearl of Great Price,* Joseph Smith 2:68-71.

to be his mission. His mission was to call Israel to repentance. When an Israelite repented under his preaching, he baptized that one. He insisted that they "bring forth therefore fruits worthy of repentance" (Luke 3:8). He did not administer the baptism of the Holy Ghost as the Mormon priests claim to do.

His final climactic ministry was that of baptizing the Lord Jesus, not for the remission of His sins, but as the Sin-bearer who would take away the sin of the world. John then made the public announcement, "Behold the Lamb of God, which taketh away the sin of the world" (John 1:29). With that, the ministry of John ended. His final message, recorded in John 3:36, he would have given to Smith and Cowdery, if he had visited them: "He that believeth on the Son hath everlasting life: and he that believeth not the Son shall not see life; but the wrath of God abideth on him."

John the Baptist, if he had been a priest of the order of Aaron, could not have ordained Smith and Cowdery to the Aaronic priesthood. Only the high priest could have done that, and then it would have to have been accompanied by a public ritual with the entire congregation present to witness the event. There would have to have been a blood sacrifice offered for the rite of sanctifying the candidates to the priesthood. In the case of Smith and Cowdery, there were no witnesses, no public ritual, and no blood sacrifice offered. All we have is their own word that they were visited by an angel, or John the Baptist; and Cowdery admitted later that the voice of John the Baptist sounded like the voice of Sidney Rigdon. It undoubtedly was.

Smith and Cowdery were not eligible for the

Aaronic priesthood. Only Israelites of the tribe of Levi and of the house of Aaron could be ordained to the Aaronic priesthood. Even then, they would have to demonstrate that their genealogy was complete.

The Melchizedek priesthood, claimed by the Mormons as their higher priesthood, is mentioned in Smith's story.

> The messenger who visited us on this occasion and conferred this Priesthood upon us, said that his name was John, the same that is called John the Baptist in the New Testament, and that he acted under the direction of Peter, James and John, who held the keys of the Priesthood of Melchizedek, which Priesthood, he said, would in due time be conferred on us, and that I should be called the first Elder of the Church, and he (Oliver Cowdery) the second. It was on the fifteenth day of May, 1829, that we were ordained under the hand of this messenger, and baptized.[2]

There is much of evasion, possibly chicanery, in the recording of the details of the priesthood. There is no date given for the visit of Peter, James, and John to bestow the Melchizedek priesthood and, obviously, no witnesses to the event. The episode is told in chapter 24 of the *Book of Commandments*, which later became *The Doctrine and Covenants*, but no mention is made of Smith and Cowdery being ordained to a priesthood. LaMar Peterson states:

> The important details that are missing from the "full history" of 1834 are likewise missing from the *Book of Commandments* in 1833. The student would expect to find all the particulars of the Restoration in the first treasured set of 65 revelations, the dates of

2. Ibid., 2:72.

which encompassed the bestowals of the two Priesthoods, but they are conspicuously absent. . . . The
notable revelations on Priesthood in the *Doctrine and
Covenants* before referred to, Sections 2 and 13, are
missing, and Chapter 28 gives no hint of the Restoration which, if actual, had been known for four years.
More than four hundred words were added to this
revelation of August, 1829 in Section 27 of the *Doctrine and Covenants,* and additions made to include
the names of heavenly visitors and two separate ordi-
nations. The *Book of Commandments* gives the duties
of Elders, Priests, Teachers, and Deacons and refers to
Joseph's apostolic calling but there is no mention of
Melchizedek Priesthood, High Priesthood, Seventies,
High Priests, or High Councilors. These words were
later inserted into the revelation on Church organization and government of April, 1830, making it appear
that they were known at that date, but they do not
appear in the original, Chapter 24 of the *Book of
Commandments,* three years later.[3]

David Whitmer, who was with Joseph Smith and
Oliver Cowdery from the beginning and was one of
the three witnesses to the golden plates, says that
there was no mention of priesthoods from the time of
the "finding" of the golden plates in 1827 until two
years after the founding of the church. He claims that
Sidney Rigdon insisted on the formation of the
priesthoods.

The Mormons are obsessed with the need for an
apostolic succession. They claim that the early
Church forfeited its charter soon after the death of the
New Testament apostles. In order to meet this need,

---

3. LaMar Peterson, *Problems in the Mormon Text,* pp. 7-8.

they felt that it was necessary for them to create a new apostolate on which to base their claim to authority.

It is their claim, which Joseph Smith wrote into his pseudoscriptures, that there was an unbroken line of those holding the priesthood, from Adam through Enoch, Melchizedek, and Abraham, and on down to New Testament times. They also claim that their gospel of repentance and baptism for the remission of sins was known and practiced from Adam down to apostolic times. Smith, in his *Inspired Version*, even has John 1:1-4 distorted to read:

> In the beginning was the gospel preached through the Son. And the gospel was the word, and the word was with the Son, and the Son was with God. . . . In him was the gospel, and the gospel was the life, and the life was the light of men.[4]

Peter, James, and John were chosen, in the Mormon scheme of priesthood, to ordain Joseph Smith and Oliver Cowdery to the Melchizedek priesthood. This, they claim, was done sometime between 1830 and 1833, with no place or time stated and with no witnesses present. The episode was written into an 1830 portion of *The Doctrine and Covenants*, Section 27. About 420 words were added to this section, possibly three years after the revelation was given, with no footnote explaining the addition.

Joseph Smith needed documentation for his adoption of the name "Melchizedek" for his higher priesthood. Therefore, in his *Inspired Version*, he augmented the story of Melchizedek by about 470 words, calculated to enlighten us on the personal back-

---

4. Joseph Smith, *Inspired Version*, John 1:1-4.

ground of Melchizedek and to explain his priesthood from Adam to the present. Here is a sampling of the material added to the story in Genesis:

> And Melchizedek lifted up his voice and blessed Abraham. Now Melchizedek was a man of faith, who wrought righteousness; and when a child he feared God, and stopped the mouths of lions, and quenched the violence of fire. And thus, having been approved of God, he was ordained an high priest after the order of the covenant which God made with Enoch. It being after the order of the Son of God. . . . And men having this faith, coming up unto this order of God, were translated and taken up to heaven. And now, Melchizedek was a priest of this order; therefore he obtained peace in Salem, and was called the Prince of peace.[5]

In the epistle to the Hebrews, Smith tampers with the reference to Melchizedek. He encloses verses 7 and 8 of chapter 5 in parentheses, making the verse apply to Melchizedek instead of to the Lord Jesus; and in chapter 7, he adds significantly to verse 3, making the Mormon priests of equal status with the Lord Jesus in the priesthood. The portions in brackets were added by Smith:

> [For this Melchizedek was ordained a priest after the order of the Son of God, which order was] without father, without mother, without descent, having neither beginning of days, nor end of life. [And all those who are ordained unto this priesthood are] made like unto the Son of God, abiding a priest continually.[6]

5. Ibid., Genesis 14:25-33.
6. Ibid., Hebrews 7:3.

By these additions and enlargements of the story of Melchizedek, Smith destroys the whole import of the priesthood of Melchizedek. The very brevity of the biblical record is the key to its significance. Melchizedek appears abruptly to Abraham, without antecedents; he blesses Abraham and receives tithes of him; and then he retreats from the picture. The writer of Hebrews uses this timelessness as symbolic of the timelessness of the priestly ministry of the Lord Jesus. It provides the great contrast with the Aaronic priesthood, which lasted as long as the priest lived and then was passed on to another for as long as he lived.

The priesthood of the Lord Jesus is unique. He offered the one sacrifice that could forever put away sin. With the sacrificial offering at Calvary, God terminated the perpetual offering of animal sacrifices (which were only types of the true sacrifice) and ended the Aaronic priesthood. Now the Offerer and the Sacrifice at Calvary established the new priesthood of the Lord Jesus; and, "seeing he ever liveth" (Hebrews 7:25), He alone has the Melchizedek priesthood, because He is not a dying priest.

The Mormons cannot have an Aaronic priesthood because they have no one who can qualify as a known son of Levi and they have no acceptable altar on which to offer a blood sacrifice. And certainly there is no need for another sacrifice.

They have no Melchizedek priesthood for the simple reason that Mormons die like other people and the Melchizedek priest never dies.

Obviously, the Mormon church has a perfect right to establish an organization and call it a priesthood instead of a board of directors, but call it what they

will, they have no moral right to claim the distinction
of having a priesthood that is directly descended from
the early Christian Church. The apostolic Church had
no priesthood. Peter, James, and John were not priests
and were not of the priestly tribe. They certainly were
not capable of ordaining anyone to any priesthood.

Smith and Cowdery were both of English ancestry
and while Joseph Smith claimed to have descended,
spiritually at least, from Joseph the son of Israel, he
still would not have qualified, because the sons of
Joseph could not serve in the priesthood. If John the
Baptist had received a commission to ordain candidates to the Aaronic priesthood, instead of going to
nothern New York State, he more likely would have
gone to New York City to seek for candidates by the
name of Cohen, who, if their lineage was correctly
descended, would have been of the house of Levi.

Finally, the Aaronic or Levitical priesthood was
terminated when the Lord Jesus offered Himself on
the cross as the "one sacrifice for sins for ever" (Hebrews 10:12). According to Paul, "the law was our
schoolmaster to bring us unto Christ, that we might be
justified by faith" (Galatians 3:24). When the Law had
fulfilled this function, its work, as administered by
the Aaronic priesthood, was completed. To reactivate
the Aaronic priesthood, as Joseph Smith claimed to
do, was blasphemy and of the apostasy of Hebrews
6:6, which crucified "the Son of God afresh, and put
him to an open shame."

There is additional material on the priesthood in
the chapter on Mormon temples.

11

The Mormons and Baptism

One of Joseph Smith's excuses for not uniting with any of the Christian churches of his day was that they were not united in their views on baptism.

He was "stumbled" because the Presbyterians and Methodists sprinkled infants or grown-ups. The Baptists immersed only responsible believers. The Friends did not baptize at all. This was also the period in which Alexander Campbell was in the process of gathering a following. The Campbellites insisted that baptism by immersion was necessary for salvation.

Smith professed to have great distress over the subject, so since his new church was in process of being founded, it was to be expected that he would arrive at a decision regarding baptism. Smith relates that while he and Oliver Cowdery were translating the golden plates, they came across mention of "baptism for the remission of sins."

Forthwith, Smith and Cowdery went into the woods to pray. Here they were met by a messenger from heaven who turned out to be John the Baptist. He announced that he was about to confer upon them the priesthood of the Aaronic order. Smith was ordered to baptize Cowdery, and Cowdery, in turn, to baptize

Smith. This accomplished, they were told that the
Melchizedek priesthood would be conferred later by
Peter, James, and John, who held this authority.[1] This
occurred on May 15, 1828. By April, 1830 *The Book of
Mormon* had been published, and the new church
organized.

By November of the same year, the church had
acquired a theologian in the person of Sidney Rigdon.
Rigdon was originally a Baptist who later followed
Alexander Campbell and adopted his views on baptismal regeneration. He broke with Campbell when
the latter failed to adopt Rigdon's ideas of communal
living. Rigdon had established a following at Kirtland, Ohio, where the principle of holding all things
in common was practiced. His new church, apart
from this communistic feature, followed closely the
teaching of Campbell. The break came in August,
1830.

There is a gap in the record of Rigdon's activities for
the next few months. One incident during this period
was the conversion of Parley Pratt under the teaching
of Rigdon. Within three weeks of his conversion, he
traveled east to New York State, as an evangelist,
where he was reconverted to Mormonism under the
preaching of Hyrum Smith, Joseph's brother.

Oliver Cowdery, Parley Pratt, and two companions
were sent west by Smith to sell *The Book of Mormon*
and to preach to the Indians. In a matter of days, they
visited Rigdon in Mentor, Ohio, and presented him
with a *Book of Mormon*. Within two weeks (mid-
November, 1830), Rigdon and his entire communal

---

1. Joseph Smith, *Pearl of Great Price*, Joseph Smith 2:68-72.

colony had accepted Mormonism and were baptized by Cowdery.

There seems to be no doubt that Joseph Smith's views on baptism were really those of Rigdon. There is good evidence (if circumstantial) that Rigdon could have been in touch with Smith during a considerable part of the developmental period of the church, as well as the period of the writing of *The Book of Mormon*. The calendar of Rigdon's life shows no entry for two months between June and August, 1828, nor for the months between October 13, 1828, and January 1, 1829. It was during this period that the manuscript of *The Book of Mormon* was progressing rapidly.

There is a gap from May until July, 1829. It was during this interval that Smith and Cowdery baptized each other, on the instructions of John the Baptist. Oliver Cowdery later commented that the voice of John the Baptist sounded amazingly like that of Elder Rigdon.[2] It probably was.

During one of these absences of Rigdon from his home, one of the most important sections of *The Doctrines and Covenants* was prepared. This is Section 20, which bears the date of April, 1830. It has complete instructions for the ordinance of baptism, the organization of the church, and the duties of church officers. This was not prepared by a novice, but by one who knew all of the practices of the church of that day. In most of its details, it parallels the policy of the early Campbellite churches with which Rigdon was familiar and in which he had been a leader.

---

2. Oliver Cowdery, *Defense: In a Rehearsal of My Grounds for Separating Myself from the Latter-Day Saints*, p. 2.

It has too much biblical content to have been written by Smith or Cowdery, unaided. Smith, by the
admission of his family, was almost totally ignorant
of the Bible in that period of his life.[3]

The story of Rigdon's conversion to Mormonism, as
given by the Mormons, is that he accepted *The Book
of Mormon* with gladness the first time it was presented to him and without having had opportunity to
give it more than a cursory examination. The gentile
version of the story is that Rigdon had been in contact
with Smith during the period of the writing of the
book. Some insist that it was he who made Solomon
Spalding's *Manuscript Found* available to Smith.

Practically all of Smith's pronouncements were
given in the form of "revelations." This is true even in
the directives on purely mundane matters. There are
abundant references to baptism and baptismal regeneration in all of his writings. *The Book of Mormon*
contains 144 references to baptism. In one such reference, 1 Nephi 10:7-19, Lehi, a Jew living in Jerusalem
in 600 B.C., prophesies in King James Version
phraseology the exact sequence of the baptism of the
Saviour by John the Baptist as related in the gospels.
The references to baptism increase in volume toward
the latter part of *The Book of Mormon,* and it is here
that the typical Rigdonian doctrines develop.

The most amazing reference, however, and the earliest in time sequence (although not revealed until at
least five years after the completion of *The Book of
Mormon*), is an elaborate record of the baptism by
immersion of Adam!

> [God] called upon . . . Adam . . . saying: . . . If thou
> wilt turn unto me . . . and believe and repent of all thy
> transgressions, and be baptized, even in water, in the
> name of mine Only Begotten Son, who is full of grace
> and truth, which is Jesus Christ . . . ye shall receive the
> gift of the Holy Ghost. . . . And our father Adam spake
> unto the Lord, and said: Why is it that men must
> repent and be baptized in water? And the Lord said
> unto Adam: Behold I have forgiven thee thy trans-
> gression in the Garden of Eden. . . . And now, behold, I
> say unto you: This is the plan of salvation unto all
> men, through the blood of mine Only Begotten, who
> shall come in the meridian of time. . . . And it came to
> pass, when the Lord had spoken with Adam, our
> father, that Adam cried unto the Lord, and he was
> caught away by the Spirit of the Lord, and was carried
> down into the water, and was laid under the water,
> and was brought forth out of the water. And thus he
> was baptized, and the Spirit of God descended upon
> him, and thus he was born of the Spirit, and became
> quickened in the inner man. And he heard a voice out
> of heaven, saying: Thou art baptized with fire, and
> with the Holy Ghost.[4]

There are thirty-eight references to baptism in *The
Doctrines and Covenants*. One of these establishes the
age at which the ordinance shall be administered:

> And their children shall be baptized for the remis-
> sion of their sins when eight years old, and receive the
> laying on of hands.[5]

It will be agreed by all Mormon theologians that
they teach unreservedly that there is no salvation in

---

4. Joseph Smith, *Pearl of Great Price*, Moses 6:51-66.
5. Joseph Smith, *Doctrine and Covenants*, 68:27.

any age—past, present, or future—apart from water
baptism. They do not even exempt from this law the
thief on the cross who was told that he would be with
the Saviour that day in paradise.

They insist that remission of sins is gained by the
administration of baptism by an authorized person,
and in this act the Holy Spirit is administered to the
candidate. This is the total formula in connection
with the "acceptance of the candidate into the Kingdom of God." In all of this, they are forced to the
admission that they consider the formula of baptism
for the remission of sins to be the process by which
salvation is initiated.

This is completely at variance with biblical teaching. Baptism for the remission of sins and salvation
from the penalty of sin are completely different propositions. An examination of the meaning of the term
and its various usages in the New Testament will
demonstrate this. The word for "remission" in Greek
is *aphesis*. It can be, and is, translated by the English
words *freedom, deliverance, forgiveness,* and *liberty,*
or the expressions *to send away, to lay aside, to remit,
to omit, to put away.* In classical Greek, it is used for
such situations as dismissing a freed slave, exempt-
ing from obligation, passing by, or ignoring.

Regarding remission of sins, the term is used in the
New Testament in two sequences in connection with
baptism. The first of these relates to the baptism of
John.

> John did baptize in the wilderness, and preach the
> baptism of repentance for the remission of sins (Mark
> 1:4).

> And he came into all the country about Jordan,
> preaching the baptism of repentance for the remission
> of sins (Luke 3:3).

This was not a case of baptism following individual
conversion, but rather of mass national repentance in
preparation for the coming of the Messiah. This was
not Christian baptism.

The second instance is in Acts 2:38, concerning the
repentant Jews at Pentecost. Peter told the people,

> Repent, and be baptized every one of you in the name
> of Jesus Christ for the remission of sins.

This passage has caused a great deal of confusion
regarding the relation between repentance and baptism. The famous Greek scholar A. T. Robertson ex-
plains how the problem is easily resolved in the Greek
text. It should read, "You (plural) repent and let each
of you (singular) be baptized." "This change marks a
break in the thought here that the English translation
does not preserve. The first thing to do is to make a
radical and complete change of heart and life. Then
let each one be baptized after this change has taken
place, and the act of baptism be performed 'in the
name of Jesus Christ.' "[6]

We find that remission of sins is more often discussed apart from baptism than with it. Hebrews 9:22
tells us that "without shedding of blood is no remission [forgiveness]." This thought is also presented in
Matthew 26:28, at the institution of the Lord's Supper. The Saviour says, "This is my blood of the new
testament [covenant], which is shed for many for the

6. A. T. Robertson, *Word Pictures in the New Testament* 3:34-35.

remission of sins." While baptism is a symbol of the
cleansing away of sins, only the "blood of Christ"
applied to the sinner can make provision for the remission of sins.

When Peter was preaching to the household of Cor-
nelius, he said, "Whosoever believeth in him shall
receive remission of sins" (Acts 10:43). In this context, remission of sins depends simply on accepting
the Saviour by faith.

There is no contradiction in the three propositions.
(1) The blood of Christ makes remission of sins possible; (2) belief in the Lord Jesus makes it available; and
(3) baptism in the name of the Lord Jesus makes a
demonstration of it.

The Greek word for "remission," *aphesis*, is used in
a number of connections in the New Testament. For
instance, it is used in the Lord's Prayer as *forgive*.
Matthew 6:12 reads: "Forgive us our debts, as we
forgive our debtors," or "remit our debts." In
Matthew 18:21, Peter asks the Saviour, "How oft shall
my brother sin against me, and I forgive him? Till
seven times?" The Lord replies: "I say not . . . Until
seven times: but, Until seventy times seven." Here the
word *forgive* or *remit* has to do with the dismissal of
our brother's offense from our minds and from the
record. It has no connection with the cleansing of the
sin in God's sight, something that must be effected
between God and the individual on the basis of the
cleansing of sin by means of Calvary. This is developed in John's first epistle.

The Mormons pursue their argument for salvation
by baptism by insisting that certain other Scriptures
refer to water baptism. They insist, for instance, that

when Paul writes to the Ephesians concerning the Church—"that he might . . . cleanse it with the washing of water by the word" (5:26)—he is speaking of water baptism.

One of the critical passages is John 3:5: "Except a man be born of water and of the Spirit, he cannot enter into the kingdom of God." There are two common interpretations of this passage: (1) the water refers to the cleansing effect of the Word of God, or (2) the water is a representation of the Spirit—that is, "born of water, even the Spirit." The latter view is possible from the Greek text, and John 7:37-39 lends additional support. Which ever of these views is held, John 3:16 clearly states that faith alone secures salvation.

> For God so loved the world, that he gave his only begotten Son, that whosoever believeth in him should not perish, but have everlasting life.

This negates the efficaciousness of water baptism for obtaining eternal life.

Titus 3:5 says, "Not by works of righteousness which we have done, but according to his mercy he saved us, by the washing of regeneration, and renewing of the Holy Ghost." The Mormons take "washing of regeneration" to mean ceremonial, water baptism, necessary for salvation. It is a reference to baptism, but it is the baptism of the Spirit, whereby He places the believer into the Body of Christ at the moment of belief. This is made clear in Romans 6:3-6, where baptism "is the picture or symbol of the new birth, not the means of securing it."[7]

7. Ibid., 4:607.

The Mormons lay much stress on the authority of their priests to baptize for the remission of sins. They insist that, in this era, only they have this authority and that it was given to them on May 15, 1829, by John the Baptist. Let us look at the record.

On that significant occasion, Joseph Smith and Oliver Cowdery were instructed to baptize each other. The messenger identified himself as John the Baptist.

Here are some problems. According to Scripture, the resurrection has not yet taken place, thus John the Baptist is still in the grave. There is no evidence that he reappeared, as Smith claimed, as a resurrected and glorified man. John the Baptist was never given any authority to ordain anyone or confer any priesthood. This is the sole province of the Head of the Church, Jesus Christ. Yet Smith claims that John ordained him as an Aaronic priest at his baptism.

Whoever it was that appeared to Smith and Cowdery—if anyone did—was obviously an imposter. Furthermore, Joseph Smith was baptized by Oliver Cowdery, who soon became an apostate, according to Smith's own testimony. Joseph Smith's authority is thus seen to be based on an unbiblical proposition, administered by an apostate, on the instructions of an imposter.

12

The Mormons and Baptism
for the Dead

Mormon doctrine insists that there is no salvation except by baptism by immersion, administered by a qualified Mormon priest. Mormons extend the teaching to include all of the millions who have lived and died on the earth without receiving a knowledge of the "restored gospel" as it was revealed to Joseph Smith.

This reasoning could only result, sooner or later, in the formulation of a doctrine of baptism for the dead. Not that the person who is baptized by proxy is saved, but that he will have another chance, after his resurrection, to hear and accept the Mormon gospel.

Apparently the doctrine was first declared in 1841,[1] for that is when it is first mentioned in exact terms. Later teachers associate it with the appearance of Elijah to Joseph Smith and Oliver Cowdery in Kirtland, Ohio, on April 3, 1836.[2] Milton Hunter comments on these circumstances.

1. Joseph Smith, *Doctrine and Covenants*, sec. 128.
2. Ibid., sec. 110.

A week following the dedication of the Kirtland Temple, April 3, 1836, Elijah appeared to Joseph Smith and Oliver Cowdery in the temple and bestowed upon them the keys of sealing power, that all the ordinances for the dead might be performed in a valid way.[3]

Apparently the ordinance was not initiated during the Kirtland days since there is no record of baptisms having been performed for the dead until the installation of the baptismal font in the partially completed Nauvoo temple. After the death of Smith and the departure of the saints from Nauvoo, the practice was not resumed until the erection of the temple in Salt Lake City.

Of course, Mormon teachers insist that baptism for the dead was always practiced by the true church, and that the true church, as it was restored by Joseph Smith, existed from the time of Adam. Smith, writing to the church on September 6, 1842, speaks of the rite as "the ordinance . . . that the Lord ordained and prepared before the foundation of the world, for the salvation of the dead who should die without a knowledge of the gospel."[4]

In the same revelation, Joseph insists that the books that will be opened at the judgment of the great white throne (Revelation 20:12) are the records of baptisms and other rites, maintained by official secretaries, in connection with the "temple work."[5]

In *The Gospel Through the Ages*, one of the current texts for the instruction of the Melchizedek priest-

3. Milton R. Hunter, *The Gospel Through the Ages*, p. 224.
4. Joseph Smith, *Doctrine and Covenants*, 128:5.
5. Ibid., 128:6-9.

hood, Milton Hunter brings Joseph Smith's teachings up-to-date. He says,

> God not only revealed the doctrine of baptism for the living to the Prophet Joseph Smith but He established on earth again the glorious doctrine of baptism for the dead, thereby opening the door to all of His sons and daughters who have ever lived in mortality to come back into His presence on condition of their worthiness. The Lord told Joseph that baptism for the dead should be performed in His holy house; in fact, one of the principle purposes He had in mind in commanding the Latter-day Saints to build temples was for the performance of the holy ordinance. In the revelation the Lord declared: "For a baptismal font there is not upon the earth, that they, my saints, may be baptized for those who are dead."
>
> Then God commanded the saints to build temples in which to perform the ordinance of baptizing for the dead, proclaiming that this ordinance was instituted before the foundation of the world for the salvation of His children who, for various reasons, would not accept the Gospel while in mortality.[6]

That none are exempt from this ordinance is made clear by James Talmage when he cites the case of the repentant malefactor who was crucified with the Lord Jesus.

> To infer that the crucified transgressor was saved by his dying confession, and was granted a special passport to Heaven with sins unexpiated and without his compliance with the "laws and ordinances of the Gospel" is to disregard both letter and spirit of scripture, and to ignore both reason and the sense of

6. Hunter, pp. 223-24.

justice—the blessing promised him was to the effect
that he should that day hear the gospel preached in
Paradise.* In the acceptance or rejection of the message of salvation he would be left an agent to himself.
The requirement of obedience to "the laws and ordinances of the Gospel" was not waived, suspended or
superseded in his case nor shall it be for any soul.[7]

The doctrine is defended as being scriptural by
using Paul's reference to the practice: "What shall
they do which are baptized for the dead, if the dead
rise not at all? why are they then baptized for the
dead?" (1 Corinthians 15:29).

Paul was not here discussing the subject of baptism
or salvation, but resurrection. Baptism for the dead
was practiced only by heretical sects, such as the
Marcionites and Montanists, and was forbidden in
A.D. 393 by the Council of Hippo. Regarding Paul's
statement, A. F. Plummer states:

> The reference is clearly to something abnormal.
> There was some baptismal rite known to the Corin-
> thians which would be meaningless without a belief
> in the resurrection. The passage does not imply that
> Saint Paul approves of the abnormal rite, but simply
> that it exists and implies the doctrine of the resurrec-
> tion.[8]

Mormons are constantly doing "work for the dead"
by compiling genealogies of their ancestors and other
notables and then being baptized for them. The Mormons are very serious about all of this. One Mormon

---

* Mormons teach that Jesus preached the Gospel to all the dead
  during the three days between His death and resurrection. The
  repentant ones of these dead must then be baptized by proxy.
  They use 1 Peter 3:19 as their proof text.

7. James E. Talmage, *Vitality of Mormonism*, pp. 70-71.
8. James Hastings, *Dictionary of the Bible*, p. 245.

admitted to me that he had been baptized over five thousand times for the dead.

This is, without doubt, the most widespread activity of the Mormon church and is one of the chief purposes of the magnificent new temples in Los Angeles and Washington, D. C. Mormons claim that these temples have been built to last throughout the Millennium and that during the thousand-year period, they will proceed to baptize, by proxy, all of the dead of the past ages who have not had a chance to respond to Smith's "restored gospel."

It would require the most highly developed computing device to calculate the total number of those in all of the ages of mankind's history who have never even heard of Joseph Smith. Also, we predict that the total would be too stupendous to be accommodated by a thousand Mormon temples such as the one in Los Angeles.

One searches the Scriptures in vain for any suggestion that those who have died out of Christ are to receive a second chance for salvation. Scripture is definite concerning the fate of those who have rejected the Saviour. We read,

> It is appointed unto men once to die, but after this the judgment (Hebrews 9:27).

> I saw the dead, small and great, stand before God; and the books were opened: and another book was opened, which is the book of life. . . . And whosoever was not found written in the book of life was cast into the lake of fire (Revelation 20:12, 15).

No greater authority can be quoted than the Lord Jesus. In the story of the rich man and Lazarus, He describes with vivid detail the fixity of the condition of those in death. Read carefully Luke 16:19-31.

One also searches in vain for any Scripture that would indicate that man is to be saved by his own good works or by the works of others, performed in his behalf. We do read, however,

> To him that worketh not, but believeth on him that justifieth the ungodly, his faith is counted for righteousness (Romans 4:5).

> By grace are ye saved through faith; and that not of yourselves: it is the gift of God: not of works, lest any man should boast (Ephesians 2:8-9).

For the benefit of any Mormon who reads these pages: these verses are rendered identically in the King James Version and in Joseph Smith's *Inspired Version* of the Bible.

13

Salvation

Joseph Smith, in his claimed interview with the Father and the Son on the occasion of the "first vision," was told that all of the churches were wrong, that their creeds were an abomination, and that their followers were all corrupt. In these three statements, Smith disposed of all the statements and restatements of the Gospel of Jesus Christ that have been preached by the Church, from apostolic days until the date of the vision in A.D. 1820.

On September 21, 1823, a heavenly messenger, Moroni, appeared to Joseph, at night in his bedroom, and told him a book was to be delivered to him that contained "the fullness of the everlasting gospel" as it had been delivered to the ancient inhabitants of America.

On April 7, 1829, John the Baptist, as an angel, appeared to Joseph Smith and Oliver Cowdery and ordered them to baptize each other. He ordained Joseph Smith as first elder of the restored church and Cowdery as second elder.

In September, 1830, Oliver Cowdery (who had ambitions) was told in a revelation, "Verily, verily I say

unto thee, no one shall be appointed to receive commandments and revelations in this church excepting
my servant, Joseph Smith, Jun., for he receiveth them
even as Moses."[1]

This series of events and pronouncements established Joseph Smith as the receiver and transmitter of
a new book of covenant doctrine, *The Book of Mormon*, and made him the supreme elder of the new
church and the only one who had the right to receive
revelations from God.

The Book of Mormon had not yet been produced
when the *Book of Commandments*, later revised as
The Doctrine and Covenants, was begun. In the introduction to section 1 of *The Doctrine and Covenants*,
dated November 1, 1831, the editors state,

> This Section constitutes the Lord's Preface to the
> doctrines, covenants, and commandments given in
> this dispensation.—Proclamation of warnings and
> commandment to the Church and to the inhabitants of
> the earth at large—The authority of the Priesthood in
> this dispensation attested—Second advent of the
> Lord Jesus Christ foretold—Authenticity of the Book
> of Mormon affirmed.[2]

In this section, given by Joseph Smith as a revelation from God, we read,

> I the Lord, knowing the calamity which should
> come upon the inhabitants of the earth, called upon
> my servant Joseph Smith, Jun., and spake unto him
> from heaven, and gave him commandments. . . . And
> after having received the record of the Nephites, yea,

---

1. Joseph Smith, *Doctrine and Covenants*, 28:2.
2. Ibid., sec. 1 (heading).

even my servant Joseph Smith, Jun., might have power to translate through the mercy of God, by the power of God, the Book of Mormon. And also those to whom these commandments are given, might have power to lay the foundation of this church, and to bring it forth out of obscurity and out of darkness, the only true and living church . . . with which I, the Lord, am well pleased, speaking unto the church collectively and not individually.[3]

With such stupendous claims and such exclusive authority, and with a direct voice from the Lord through His servant, Joseph Smith, Jun., one would expect a pronouncement of a gospel that would be vitally new, especially after an apostasy of seventeen hundred years. We should at least find a definitive statement of what the gospel is. What does Smith tell us?

If thou wilt do good, yea, and hold out faithful to the end, thou shalt be saved in the kingdom of God, which is the greatest of all the gifts of God; for there is no gift greater than the gift of salvation.[4]

And, if you keep my commandments and endure to the end you shall have eternal life, which gift is the greatest of all the gifts of God.[5]

And as many as repent and are baptized in my name, which is Jesus Christ, and endure to the end, the same shall be saved.[6]

That as many as would believe and be baptized in

3. Ibid., 1:17, 29, 30.
4. Ibid., 6:13.
5. Ibid., 14:7.
6. Ibid., 18:22.

his holy name, and endure in faith to the end, should be saved.[7]

> Yea, repent and be baptized, every one of you, for a remission of your sins; yea, be baptized even in water, and then cometh the baptism of fire and of the Holy Ghost.
> Behold, verily, verily, I say unto you, this is my gospel; and remember that they shall have faith in me or they can no wise be saved;
> And upon this rock I will build my church; yea, upon this rock ye are built, and if ye continue, the gates of hell shall not prevail against you.[8]

After reading Ephesians 2:8-9, in the King James Version of the Bible, and disagreeing with it, one of the ancient scribes of *The Book of Mormon*, Nephi, writes, "For we know that it is by grace that we are saved, after all we can do."[9]

After examining Smith's presentation of such a gospel, we realize that the above statements are such as any of Smith's contemporaries could have heard from the lips of any uneducated, ignorant exhorter of the day. Even Alexander Campbell, who insisted on baptism accompanying salvation, required a repentance and conversion experience. Smith's formula is not remotely the Gospel of the grace of God. The entire message of the Mormon writings is one of good works, baptism, and complete loyalty to Joseph Smith and his successors, with practically no mention of the Lord Jesus as Saviour. In 1857, Brigham Young said,

> I want you to tell them, and tell all the great men of

---

7. Ibid., 20:25.
8. Ibid., 33:11-13.
9. Joseph Smith, *Book of Mormon*, 2 Nephi 25:23.

the earth, that the Latter-day Saints are to be their redeemer. . . . Believe in God, believe in Jesus, and believe in Joseph his Prophet, and in Brigham his successor, and I add, "If you will believe in your hearts and confess with your mouth Jesus is the Christ, that Joseph was a prophet, and that Brigham is his successor, you shall be saved in the Kingdom of God."[10]

He also said,

No man or woman in this dispensation will ever enter into the celestial kingdom of God without the consent of Joseph Smith . . . every man and woman must have the certificate of Joseph Smith, junior, as a passport to their entrance into the mansions where God and Christ are—I cannot go there without his consent . . . he reigns there as supreme a being in his sphere, capacity, and calling, as God does in heaven.[11]

Joseph Fielding Smith, the tenth president of the Mormon church, wrote,

No salvation without accepting Joseph Smith. If Joseph Smith was verily a prophet, and if he told the truth . . . then this knowledge is of the most vital importance to the entire world. No man can reject that testimony without incurring the most dreadful consequences, for he cannot enter the Kingdom of God.[12]

In giving their "witness," the young Mormon missionaries invariably assure their hearers that they believe that *The Book of Mormon* is the word of God and

10. Brigham Young, in *Journal of Discourses* 6:229.
11. Ibid., 7:289.
12. Joseph Fielding Smith, *Doctrines of Salvation*, pp. 189-90.

that Joseph Smith was the prophét of God. You will never hear them say that they know that their sins are forgiven or that they have eternal life because they have believed in the Lord Jesus Christ for their salvation.

Joseph Smith insisted that "many precious portions" had been removed from the original Scriptures, and many had been mistranslated, and for this reason we needed new scriptures. The following precious portions were not deleted or changed and, in fact, are in Joseph Smith's *Inspired Version*, unchanged from the King James Version.

> By grace are ye saved through faith; and that not of yourselves: it is the gift of God: not of works, lest any man should boast (Ephesians 2:8-9).

> Jesus Christ of Nazareth. . . . Neither is there salvation in any other: for there is none other name under heaven given among men, whereby we must be saved (Acts 4:10-12).

> That if thou shalt confess with thy mouth the Lord Jesus, and shalt believe in thine heart that God hath raised him from the dead, thou shalt be saved (Romans 10:9).

In order to make a comparison of salvation as a Mormon sees it and salvation as it is accepted by all orthodox Christians of whatever communion, we will state the Christian view of salvation and then quote the Mormon view from writers acceptable to the Mormons. The reader may come to his own conclusions. Salvation, according to the Bible, involves a threefold deliverance.

1. Deliverance from the penalty of sin, so that the sinner stands justified before God and cleansed from the guilt of sin. This guarantees him eternal life and eternal deliverance from judgment.
2. Deliverance from the power of sin in his daily life and throughout his earthly experience as a believer. This is made possible by the presence of the indwelling Spirit of God.
3. Deliverance, eventually, from the very presence of sin, when the redeemed shall be ushered into the presence of God.

There are some slight variations in the mode of expressing these three basic benefits of salvation, but all Christians will agree that these benefits are the result of the redemptive work of Christ on Calvary. Christians will agree that the work of Calvary was substitutionary. They believe that Jesus Christ, as man's Substitute, satisfied all of God's claims against fallen man with regard to sin. The validity of this redemptive work is assured by the physical resurrection of Jesus Christ from the dead, thus evidencing His triumph over death.

Salvation, according to the Bible, is available to all, regardless of the depth to which the sinner has descended in the quantity or quality of his sins, since the work of redemption at Calvary was complete. Salvation is attained by the acceptance of God's free gift, as stated in Ephesians 2:8-9: "By grace are ye saved through faith; and that not of yourselves: it is the gift of God: not of works, lest any man should boast."

Salvation is not attained by self-effort or good works. It does, however, give the believer the ability to produce good works, not for the purpose of per-

petuating or enhancing his salvation, but because the
yearning is present, within the believer, to produce
fruit for God. One wants to perform works pleasing to
God out of a sense of love for the Saviour.

Now, contrast this Christian and biblical view of
salvation with the Mormon view. The Mormon writers borrow verses from the Bible to support their view,
but without discrimination as to the subject under
discussion in the context of that Scripture. Here is a
statement by John A. Widtsoe, who is considered by
Mormons to be among their most competent
apologists.

> What is salvation? It is the condition that results
> when a person is in harmony with truth. Man may
> ever be on the way to salvation, but in its fullness,
> salvation is the eternal goal. The law of salvation, as of
> all life, is eternal progression. One must grow daily
> and forever in righteousness and good works. Those
> who are in a state of salvation are in a constant state of
> progression. Those who are static or who retrograde
> are "the lost". Even for the latter, the tender mercy of
> God provides a fitting place in His kingdom, and the
> opportunity for continuous repentance. Whoever has
> placed himself by obedience to divine law beyond the
> power of evil, to that extent is saved.
>
> How may salvation be attained? By accepting the
> principles and practices of truth issuing from God
> and constituting the plan of salvation by the resolute
> use of the will to obey at any cost the requirements of
> the Gospel: and the constant appeal in prayer to God
> for assistance.
>
> Does Christ do something for man which man can-
> not do for himself? Yes. He is our Redeemer; he leads
> us along the dim path; his sacrifice will enable us to

recover the bodies we lay down in the grave; he is our advocate with the Father. He is our Captain.[13]

Concerning the antipathy manifested by Mormons toward the Christian view of salvation, we here quote an editorial from the church page of the *Deseret News*, the official daily newspaper of the Salt Lake Mormons.

A Two-Edged Sword

Satan is the arch-deceiver. His doctrine appears under many a guise. Always he attempts to lead people astray by holding before them false notions which on the surface seem much to be desired.

One of his most appealing methods of reaching mankind is to make them believe they can get something for nothing. Nearly everyone has enough selfishness to try to get all he can at the lowest price. Satan plays upon that trait. He does so in our economic life, and he does so in religion. Get something for nothing—or for as little as you can.

This identical philosophy is carried over into certain types of religion. Again it is to get something for nothing. Some teach that a person may have full salvation by whispering a few magic words. Just confess a belief in the Saviour—that is all. If you thus confess, you get full salvation, and nothing can keep you from it. No works are necessary, for you are saved by grace alone, so the teaching goes.

Get something—get salvation—for nothing but a phrase. Just say, "I believe". That is all there is to it, they declare. And they quote John 3:16 to support their arguments.

This unfounded fancy has become so popular with

---

13. John A. Widtsoe, *Varieties of American Religion*, pp. 137-38.

some that certain enthusiasts go to the extent of painting "John 3:16" on fences, on sign posts, on railroad overpasses, along the highways, anywhere. It is magic in their eyes, a magic way to be saved. But it is black magic, and they deceive themselves, for salvation comes not in that manner.

But is it not a striking thing that Satan would hold forth this same philosophy in both the fields of economics, or every-day bread-and-butter living, and in religion? And is it not remarkable that both these expressions of the same false philosophy are so popular with people?

The Lord has had a good deal to say about this matter, and his doctrine is just opposite to that of Lucifer. Instead of teaching us to get something for nothing, the Lord puts a premium upon production. His doctrine is that the idler shall not eat the bread nor wear the garments of the laborer.

And in religion it is the same. We are taught that we must work out our salvation. We must bring forth much fruit. Those branches of the vine which do not produce much good fruit shall be cut off and thrown into the fire. He emphasized production in his parable of the unprofitable servant. Faith without works is dead. On Judgment Day we shall be judged according to the deeds done in the body.

The Lord commands us to become perfect, even as he is. In giving us the commandment, and teaching us that we must work out our salvation, with prayer, and fasting, and increasing faith and testimony, he teaches us that we must put forth genuine effort for self-improvement.

How do we work out our salvation? By participating in the activities of the Church which develop in our souls those Christ-like traits that help us to become like him. That requires consistent, well-planned effort, with devotion to the end. So working out our salvation means developing Christ-like characters which will make us fit to come into the presence of the Lord.

Latter-day Saints should not be deceived by Satan's philosophies of getting something for nothing. That false doctrine is like a two-edged sword which destroys either way it swings, whether in economics or in religion.[14]

It is quite obvious that the benefits of salvation, according to the Mormon philosophy, would be available only to a few, well-endowed persons. There is no provision for the derelict, the mediocre, or the host of earth dwellers who would have no means or opportunity to produce the sort of effort prescribed by Mormon teachers.

By contrast the Christian message is to "whosoever will." The repentant sinner comes to Christ using the words of Augustus Toplady,

> Nothing in my hand I bring,
> Simply to Thy cross I cling.

The Mormon comes saying,

> Something in my hand I bring,
> To my own good works I cling.

Which will God accept?

---

14. *Deseret News*, January 16, 1952.

14

The Book of Mormon

Mormons become quite emotional when they tell of the innocent farm boy, Joseph Smith, who began having visions at age fourteen and at age sixteen was visited by an angel and shown the depository of a cache of golden plates, from which he would eventually translate *The Book of Mormon*.

But the farm boy was not as innocent as he is portrayed, nor was he alone in the pranks of his teen years. He was the ringleader, or at least the wizard, of a gang of young fellows who spent much time searching for buried treasure. Smith had the skill of manipulating the divining rod and the peep-stone that enabled him to detect the presence of the treasure.

His mother, in her memoirs, tells of gangs of ruffians who were chasing Joseph and trying to get hold of the golden plates after the angel Moroni had delivered them to him. The fact is that these ruffians were his old partners who felt that they should have a share in the treasure, if there was one. They probably felt that he was holding out on them.

Treasure hunting, especially in Smith's time, was a rather guileless occupation, but Smith was haled into court on the charge of being a "glass looker." He was tried, convicted, and jailed for his offense. His misdemeanor lay in the fact that he was exploiting his pretended skill and getting no results for his clients.

This trial and conviction occurred in 1826, when Smith was twenty years old—much too old to be engaged in teenage pranks of treasure hunting. It was during this period of treasure hunting that Smith claimed to have come into possession of the golden plates. He says, however, that it was an angel that revealed the location of the plates.[1]

There are so many variations in the stories surrounding the finding of the plates and hiding them from enemies, that it is impossible (and not pertinent to this book) to list them all. The Mormon versions of the story, alone, would fill a good-sized booklet and would present more problems than they would solve. The story as told by Joseph Smith's mother, Lucy, is about as weird as any and gives light on the superstitious temperament of the Smith family. This, among other stories, caused Brigham Young to suppress her book and have all copies destroyed.

Joseph was not alone in the preparation of the source material for the manuscript of *The Book of Mormon*. As for the golden plates, we will say simply that there were not any. No one ever saw them. Smith had something mysterious secreted in a box or covered with a cloth. The shape and size of this object, as described, is pictured as an arch binder about eight inches by eight inches and about four or five inches thick. A mass of gold of this size would weigh about

---

1. Jerald and Sandra Tanner, *Mormonism; Shadow or Reality*, chap. 4.

250 pounds, yet Joseph's mother describes Joseph as
running with the plates under his arm for two miles,
encountering two adversaries and knocking them
aside, and finally reaching the house—out of breath,
but, strangely enough, without the plates under his
arm![2]

Later on in the story, when Joseph is compelled to
show the plates to three witnesses and take their testimony, it was necessary for Smith to conjure up a
vision, with an angel displaying the plates and flip-
ping the pages.[3] We dismiss the story of the golden
plates as totally unnecessary and an encumbrance to
the story rather than a help.

There must have been a manuscript, or at least a
collection of notes, that went into the writing of the
book. This is not material from the fertile mind of an
ignorant farm boy. Someone has described a giraffe as
a horse put together by a committee. *The Book of
Mormon* has all the appearance of an imitation of the
Bible, put together by a committee of biblically ignorant craftsmen, who did not like the Bible because it
was too much of a challenge to their consciences.

A coterie of associates surrounded Smith in the
translation of *The Book of Mormon,* the founding of
the church, and the formulation of its doctrines. A
group of at least five men were in touch with each
other, openly or clandestinely, for a period of several
years before the book came forth.

The Mormons insist that these men did *not* know
each other before they came, one at a time, into the

2. Lucy Mack Smith, *Biographical Sketches of Joseph Smith the
   Prophet and His Progenitors for Many Generations,* pp. 104-5.
3. Gordon B. Hinckley, *What of the Mormons?,* chap. 7.

story. They are presented as a group of individuals, all with troubled minds over the condition of the church, and all obsessed with the same desire to see a New Testament Church emerge. Their paths crossed, one by one, and all became assured that Joseph Smith was indeed a prophet.

Five men entered the picture as the story progressed. *Martin Harris* was a neighboring farmer who was prosperous in business but a hopeless visionary. In his lifetime, he was a member of at least fifteen religious groups, from Universalism to Shakerism. He had the funds Smith needed for the project. *Oliver Cowdery* was a blacksmith and some-time schoolteacher. He put in his appearance ostensibly to teach school, but within a few days he was serving as Smith's scribe. *Parley Pratt* was a wandering mystic, preacher, and bookseller who was well known around Palmyra. The Mormon story has him running feverishly to Palmyra to see the young prophet so that he could hear the story firsthand. Joseph was not around, but Hyrum, Joseph's brother, converted and baptized him. *David Whitmer* was a farmer and mystic, living at Fayette, Pennsylvania, about fifty miles from where Smith and Cowdery were translating at Harmony. According to the record of Joseph's mother, persecution was beginning at Harmony and the brethren needed a new place to translate. Cowdery and Sidney Rigdon both knew the Whitmers, so, quite conveniently, Joseph received a special revelation, while they were translating, that he should write immediately to the Whitmers asking that the translating team might move in with them for the moment. *Sid-*

ney *Rigdon,* who was to become Smith's theologian,
was a well-known evangelist and exhorter, first as a
Baptist, then as an associate of Alexander Campbell.
He had left the Baptist connection and joined
Campbell for a period of nearly ten years. He was
disfellowshipped by Campbell for some extravagant
views that, curiously enough, showed up later in
Mormon teachings.

The Mormon story is that, after *The Book of Mormon* was published, Parley Pratt and Oliver Cowdery
were sent on a mission to the Indians in the West, but
showed up promptly at Rigdon's place, in northern
Ohio, where they showed him a *Book of Mormon.* At
first he feigned surprise and said that the book was of
the devil. However, within a matter of hours, he accepted the book as the word of God and, within a
two-week period, had converted his entire flock of
about 150 to Mormonism.

All of these men knew each other for a period of
years before *The Book of Mormon* was finished.
Oliver Cowdery, who knew both Pratt and Rigdon
(Pratt had been one of Rigdon's followers), came from
Poultney, Vermont, where a fellow townsman had
written a book, *View of the Hebrews,* that sought to
prove that the Indians were the lost tribes of Israel.
The book, by Ethan Smith, was published just a year
or so before Cowdery put in his appearance. Cowdery
knew the Whitmers, and the Whitmers already knew
about the plates and Nephi, one of the characters of
The Book of Mormon. Rigdon had preached throughout this part of the country for several years. According to the *History of Wayne County, New York, 1789-*

1877,[4] it was Sidney Rigdon who married Joseph Smith and Emma Hale.

Thus we have the complete committee, knowing each other in advance, but working so as to screen the operation. There was the prophet, Joseph, with his abilities as a seer of invisible things; Oliver Cowdery, the scribe, with the plot well known from Ethan Smith's volume; Martin Harris, financier of the project; David Whitmer, who would be one of the three witnesses to the golden plates; Parley Pratt, with several years of studies in mystic religions; and Sidney Rigdon, the orator, with a knowledge of the Scriptures, but with rather weird concepts of the church, and with a full knowledge of the workings of Alexander Campbell's ecclesiology. Now all they needed was the script. The following pages will give light on that part of the program.

---

4. W. H. McIntosh Everts, *History of Wayne County, New York, 1789-1877*, p. 150.

15

Lost Tribes of Israel

In the days of Joseph Smith, it was an almost universal belief that the American Indians were the lost tribes of Israel. The idea had its beginnings in the days of the Puritan migrations to Massachusetts in the seventeenth century.

When the Puritans discovered that the new land to which they had come was already populated with a distinct people who were quite different from Englishmen, they felt that they must account for them as a race. Because they were ardent believers in the Old Testament and its promises to Israel, the Puritans identified themselves as the Israel of God, now entering into the promised land. And they reasoned that the Indians were the remnant of the lost tribes of Israel. If that were so, it was the Puritans' duty, as the Israel of God, to extend the blessings of God to the Indians and make good, knowledgeable Israelites out of them. John Elliot, who translated the Bible into an Indian language, had this idea. He was a sincere believer and was anxious that the Indians should become Christians and, as Israelites, should enter into their inheritance. It may have been this idea that prompted his use of Ezekiel 37:1-14 as the text of the

130

first sermon he preached to the Indians at Nonantum. The "dry bones" of the house of Israel equated with the dry bones of these American Israelites.

This idea of the Indians as the lost tribes of Israel persisted for two hundred years. Within the three decades before the writing of *The Book of Mormon*, at least six books or papers were available to Joseph Smith and his associates that promoted the idea. Notable among these were (1) an essay by Charles Crawford, of Philadelphia, dated 1799, written "to prove that many of the Indians in America are descended from the ten tribes"; (2) *A Star in the West* (1816), by Elias Boudinot of Trenton, New Jersey, which the author describes as "a humble attempt to discover the long lost tribes of Israel"; (3) *The Wonders of Nature and Providence Displayed*, by Josiah Priest, published in Albany in 1825; and (4) *A View of the Hebrews*, published by Ethan Smith, supposedly a distant relative of Joseph Smith, and written in Poultney, Vermont, in 1823, reprinted in 1825. Oliver Cowdery, Joseph Smith's scribe, came from Poultney, Vermont, soon after the publication of Ethan Smith's volume.

All of these writers, while convinced that they were on the right track, proposed their theses as theories that seemed to indicate that this was the true origin of the Indians. Joseph Smith and his associates were not so modest. Borrowing the theories of these and other writers, they wrote a book that they made appear to be valid Scripture.

Thus *The Book of Mormon* purports to be a volume of sacred history, the only great difference being that the writers of *The Book of Mormon* made the Indians to be escaped Israelites from the Jewish captivity in

Babylon, in about 600 B.C. These escapees traveled to the west coast of America and developed the civilizations described in the book.

In defending *The Book of Mormon*, the Mormons are faced with several problems.

1. The ten tribes are not lost; they are simply not visible. God knows where they are scattered, and, in His time, He will assemble twelve thousand of each tribe (see Revelation 7).
2. The American Indians would have to be Semites, if the Mormon book is true, which they definitely are not.
3. The historical and archaeological pronouncements of *The Book of Mormon* are at complete variance with the known historical and archaeological facts relating to the natives of America. These points are discussed further in chapter 17.

Unfortunately, Smith and his associates wrote just before the studies of ancient America began. Now it is well known who was where in America at the time period of *The Book of Mormon*, and the facts just do not coincide.

The Mormon church has spent millions in trying to justify the validity of *The Book of Mormon*, but even Mormon scholars are cautioning their people about making claims. But the church must, at all cost, vindicate its prophet and his talisman, *The Book of Mormon*. If they jettisoned *The Book of Mormon*, they would unseat their prophet.

16

Outline of the Book of Mormon

For the sake of our readers who are not familiar with the story of *The Book of Mormon,* and to assure our Mormon readers that we are aware of the basic story of the book, we will outline the several migrations from the Old World to the New, as they are recorded.

We emphasize the fact that Mormons in our present day are still committed to the historical and geographical material in *The Book of Mormon.* It is taught as serious history in their schools, in their Sunday schools, and to their young missionaries.

The professors at Brigham Young University are more cautious in their claims than they were a decade ago, but some of them are still committed to vindicating *The Book of Mormon's* record.

The following is a resume, by Brigham H. Roberts, of the structure of *The Book of Mormon.*

> In this important and interesting book the history of ancient America is unfolded, from its first settlement by a colony that came from the Tower of Babel, at the confusion of languages, to the beginning of the fifth century of the Christian era. We are informed by these records that America in ancient times has been inhabited by two distinct races of people. The first were

called Jaredites and came directly from the Tower of Babel. The second came directly from the city of Jerusalem, about 600 B.C. They were principally Israelites of the descendents of Joseph. The Jaredites were destroyed about the time the Israelites came from Jerusalem, who succeeded them in the inheritance of the country.[1]

A third migration, not noted above, is recorded in *The Book of Mormon*. It took place a few years after the Nephite migration of 600 B.C. and was led by a man named Mulek. *The Book of Mormon* says Mulek was a son of Zedekiah, King of Judah.[2]

The first migration is described in extravagant detail in the Book of Ether, a section of *The Book of Mormon*. It is an amazing bit of fantasy. The second migration is described in the First Book of Nephi of *The Book of Mormon*.

Mormon apologists assure us that *The Book of Mormon* gives the only reliable history of what happened on the American continents from the time of the tower of Babel until the beginning of the fifth century of the Christian era. The whole story is told in detail, as sober history; therefore, Mormons cannot complain if we examine the credibility of the details in the light of what we now know about the inhabitants of the New World.

In *An Approach to the Book of Mormon*, a text for the training of the Melchizedek priesthood, Hugh Nibley seeks to push into a maze of obscurity the possibility of proving or disproving the various his-

1. Brigham H. Roberts, *Mormonism, Its Origin and History*, p. 15.
2. Joseph Smith, *Book of Mormon*, Mosiah 25:2; Helaman 6:10; 8:21.

torically reported episodes of *The Book of Mormon.* He says,

> There are no natural laws by which the social scientist can tell whether events and situations described in the *Book of Mormon* were real or not. All we have is a huge heap of ancient records which will indicate more or less whether such things were possible or plausible.[3]

This is wishful thinking on the part of Nibley, because there is more than a "heap of ancient records." There is the history of the Near East in secular records, as well as the one reliable Book, the Bible, with which to check the movements of the people in *The Book of Mormon,* for they migrated from Jerusalem at a time and under circumstances that are well documented. If by the "heap of ancient records" Nibley means the great amount of information gathered by anthropologists and archaeologists working in ancient American ruins, the picture is by no means obscure. Both Mormon scientists and objective investigators have reconstructed the story of who lived where in ancient America, when they occupied certain territories, what their cultures were, and, to a large degree, what their writing methods were.

Certainly these facts were not known when Joseph Smith wrote, but this gives the Mormons of today no right to suppress the information they have found or to ignore the scientific findings of others.

To challenge Nibley's philosophy concerning unidentifiable times and places, we insist that the probable accuracy of *The Book of Mormon* can be evalu-

---

3. Hugh Nibley, *An Approach to the Book of Mormon,* p. 3.

ated by an examination of the book's records of situations, times, and places that are well known and well documented.

If, for instance, the statements of history, geography, natural history, ethnology, and anthropology in *The Book of Mormon* almost invariably prove to be untrue, it is safe to assume that completely illogical statements in the rest of the book will follow the same pattern.

A sample of an impossible situation, in which time and place are definitely stated, is given in the second chapter of *The Book of Mormon*. The time is 600 B.C., the place, Jerusalem and the borders of the Red Sea. To avoid capture by the Babylonians, Lehi, a patriarch, took his family away from Jerusalem, in spite of the specific command of the Lord to the contrary.

> And it came to pass that he departed into the wilderness. And he left his house, and the land of his inheritance, and his gold, and his silver, and his precious things, and took nothing with him, save it were his family, and provisions, and tents, and departed into the wilderness.
>
> And he came down by the borders near the shore of the Red Sea; and he traveled in the wilderness in the borders which are nearer the Red Sea; and he did travel in the wilderness with his family, which consisted of my mother, Sariah, and my elder brothers, who were Laman, Lemuel and Sam.
>
> And it came to pass that when he had traveled three days in the wilderness, he pitched his tent in a valley by the side of a river of water.
>
> And it came to pass that he built an altar of stones, and made an offering unto the Lord, and gave thanks unto the Lord our God.

> And it came to pass that he called the name of the river, Laman, and it emptied into the Red Sea; and the valley was in the borders near the mouth thereof.
>
> And when my father saw that the waters of the river emptied into the fountain of the Red Sea, he spake unto Laman, saying: O that thou mightest be like unto this river, continually running into the fountain of all righteousness.[4]

In this portion of the story are a number of clearly stated details that can be used as checkpoints. (1) They left Jerusalem during Nebuchadnezzar's siege of that city. (2) They traveled on foot. If they had donkeys to carry their luggage and tents, they would still have had to walk beside the donkeys. (3) They traveled three days in the wilderness. (4) They came to a valley through which flowed a river. (5) The river ran into the Red Sea. (6) According to 1 Nephi 16:12-13, they were traveling in a "south-southeast direction."

1. According to the details given of the siege of Jerusalem, everyone who broke out to flee was overtaken and killed by the armies of Nebuchadnezzar. The escape of Lehi and his family, therefore, was highly improbable.

2. On foot or by ox cart, under good conditions, people travel at about three miles per hour. Even the more sophisticated wagon trains of the American migrations west were seldom faster than this three-mile-per-hour speed.

3. On that basis, three days' travel would have brought the pilgrims about seventy-five miles south-southeast of Jerusalem, to the southern tip of the Dead

---

4. Joseph Smith, *Book of Mormon*, 1 Nephi 2:4-9.

Sea, not the Red Sea. It would have taken them about
seven days of favorable traveling to reach the closest
tip of the Red Sea, the Gulf of Aqaba. If the three days'
journey was taken after they reached the Red Sea, they
would still have been on the coast of the Gulf of Aqaba
in the Midian Desert.

4. There are no rivers in this part of the world.

5. No rivers run into the Red Sea anywhere along
the fifteen-hundred-mile length of its western coast.

Here are one improbability and several impossibilities to quench Dr. Nibley's argument. Obviously,
Joseph Smith did not have access to an atlas of the
Near East, or he would not have fallen into a trap so
early in his story with details that can easily be
checked for accuracy.

The story continues turgidly, with the party of pilgrims traversing the Arabian Peninsula for seven
years, passing through the Rub-al-Khali Desert to the
shores of the Persian Gulf. There they reached a
"fruitful land," which they named Bountiful because
of its much fruit and honey.

Next, Nephi was instructed to construct a ship for
passage to the promised land. But he was at a point
which is probably as far from a source of shipbuilding
timber as any spot on earth. Nephi was commanded
by the Lord to come up into a mountain to obtain
instructions for building the ship, but there are no
mountains within several hundred miles of "Bountiful" on the Persian Gulf. The ship was built and, in
spite of mutinies, after many days arrived safe and
sound on the coast of America. The west coast is
usually accepted by the Mormons. No detail is given
about their transit across the Arabian Sea and the

Indian Ocean, their passage of the archipelagoes of Southeast Asia, or their crossing of the Pacific Ocean. Simply "after many days," they reached the promised land.

Seventeen chapters of *The Book of Mormon* bring the pilgrims to the promised land. They are so full of improbabilities, impossibilities, and illogical situations that we should not expect the writers of the book to improve the quality of their story when they come to a world area of which, in Joseph Smith's time, very little was known.

Now that the facts are known of the cultures, races, languages, geography, and religions of the ancient Americans, we can objectively evaluate the story of *The Book of Mormon*, as it purports to give its version. Unfortunately for it, Dr. Nibley's "heap of ancient records" has told an eloquent tale.

17

Semites in America

We do not doubt the possibility or probability of migrations across the South Pacific or of landings on the coast of Panama or Central America. The ocean currents would allow this, with a northward drift, to the southern coast of Mexico.

The old civilizations of Mexico and Central America are the ones claimed by Mormons as the people of *The Book of Mormon*, and the cities and temples of those civilizations are said to be of the Nephites and Lamanites of Smith's story. Whether Nephite or Lamanite, they would still have to be Semites.

What do the "heap of ancient records" and the vast amount of archaeological material that has been classified and deciphered tell us? Simply this. The entire area was already populated by known tribes or nations in embryo. The entire Pacific coast, from northern Mexico to the Isthmus of Tehuantepec, was occupied by the Tabascan, Mixtec, and Zapotec. The Valley of Mexico was occupied by the ancestors of the Toltec, probably the Teotihuacan. The east coast, from north to south, was occupied by the Huastec, Totonac, Olmec, and Maya.[1]

1. Victor Von Hagen, *The Aztec, Man and Tribe*, pp. 17, 28, 31.

The tribes were homogenous, sedentary, and lived by hunting, gathering the bountiful supply of nature, and cultivating known crops. Physically, they were of Mongoloid types. They were not city builders, although worship centers with pyramids and tombs came later. However, they came much later than the dates given in *The Book of Mormon*.

Here we come to some verifiable blunders in *The Book of Mormon*. Joseph Smith has the ancient Americans of his book in possession of such crops as wheat, barley, flax, and olives, none of which were known in America until the Spanish conquest. They also have horses, cattle, sheep, swine, and goats, none of which were in America until the coming of the Europeans. They have fabrics of silk, fine linen, and wool one thousand years before these items were available in America. The staples in ancient America were maize and cotton, neither of which is mentioned in *The Book of Mormon*.

Joseph Smith has the natives using a monetary system, with metallic money in gold, silver, and copper, in 82 B.C., one thousand years before any metal was used for any purpose in America. When metal *was* used, its values were the reverse of the monetary values of *The Book of Mormon*. Ancient America had no iron age, but it did have some malleable meteoric nickle-iron that was used for cutting implements. That was the most valuable metal. Copper was of great value because it could be used for tools. Silver was next, because it was more difficult to smelt and therefore not worth the effort to obtain. Gold was considered cheap metal because it had utility only for decorative purposes. The economy of ancient America

was on the basis of exchange of commodities. Any
balances in the calculation were made up by cocoa
beans.

The *Book of Mormon* has the Americans in possession of all of the metallic paraphernalia of war making. Scimitars, swords, metal shields, and chariots are
mentioned. The wheel was never used in America
and they had no beasts of burden, so the chariots and
horses were invented by Joseph Smith.

Smith has the ancient Americans engaging in mas-
sive armed conflicts, with armies of as many as two
hundred thousand engaged in single battles. By contrast, the ancient Americans were notably sedentary
and peaceful. When the Aztecs (nine hundred years
after *The Book of Mormon* dates) engaged in warfare,
they did so as an adjunct to their sun worship. Great
numbers of their enemies were captured to be sac-
rificed in daily rites to the sun god. When they engaged in trade, they combined spreading their religion and trading commercially. Their trading cara-
vans consisted of slaves, carrying the merchandise on
their backs. The tumpline—a band across the
forehead with thongs supporting the burden on the
back—was the symbol of transportation in Aztec
Mexico. These slaves carried the bulk merchandise
from the Valley of Mexico to the Mayan areas to be
traded there for more valuable, nonbulky goods. On
the return trip to Mexico fewer slaves were needed for
the more concentrated loads, so surplus slaves were
either sold or killed in order to save expenses.

The *Book of Mormon* tells of systems of government, with kings, palaces, fortresses, and armies, and

even bands of raiders and plunderers. No such things were known. The great buildings and temples always revolved around the pagan religions. Priests were the dominant ruling class, and as they became overbearing, demanding more and more of the products of the people, the citizens would revolt and destroy them.

The focal episode in the story of *The Book of Mormon* is the coming of Jesus Christ to the ancient Americans after His resurrection. He preached long sermons, retold the Sermon on the Mount, and established a church with twelve Nephite apostles, all in the pattern of the Mormon church of Joseph Smith. The church is supposed to have lasted for nearly three hundred years and, at least at one period, to have dominated the scene. It became apostate, with only a few enduring to the end.

Mormon archaeologists have been trying for years to establish some evidence that would confirm the presence of the church in America. There is still not a scintilla of evidence, either in the religious philosophy of the ancient writings or in the presence of artifacts, that could lead to such a belief.

One artifact has been heralded as an evidence of the coming of Christ to America. It has come to be known as the Temple of the Cross, located at Palenque in the State of Chiapas. In this temple is an artifact that suggests a cross, but it is in no way the cruciform of Christian art. The object, when studied carefully, turns out to be an altar to the Quetzal bird. The very elaborate transom seems to be a shelf on which the paraphernalia of the priest was placed. One of the priests in the panel seems to be offering a small child as a sacrifice.

Cross marks on the tunic of the serpent-priest Quetzalcoatl are promoted as symbols of the Christian cross. We would hasten to remind Mormons that the cross on which the Saviour died was a *palus,* or pole, without a transom member. The classical cruciform developed later in Christian art.

The final episode in *The Book of Mormon* is the climactic battle between the Nephites and the Lamanites. Moroni and his father, Mormon, are the heroes of the last chapters. Practically all of the historic part of the book takes place in Mexico and Central America. But strangely enough, the scene closes with the action taking place in Wayne and Ontario counties in western New York State. The final battles engage two hundred thousand Nephites and presumably the same number or more of the Lamanites, but the Nephites are reduced to a few individuals, one of whom is Moroni.

Moroni's last deeds include finishing the golden plates and burying them in a hillside adjacent to the Smith farm at Palmyra, New York, so that Joseph could find them fourteen hundred years later.

It is a fact that there were great pits of bones found in that part of the United States. But when the facts were understood, they indicated that the Indians of the region had ceremonies in which the accumulated bones of tribal members were brought together periodically and, with considerable ceremony, interred in communal pits. These mounds of bones and the stories of buried treasures, combined with the imagination of youth, were great material for developing such stories as are contained in *The Book of Mormon.*

The whole array of anachronisms in the book stamps it as written by someone who knew nothing about ancient America and presumed that no one ever would know. It is total fiction, done by one who assumed that cultures in ancient America would probably be about the same as those of our own north-eastern states in the nineteenth century. While certain Mormon apologists are pledged to the task of defending the credibility of *The Book of Mormon*, because the church demands it, some professors at Brigham Young University are demanding caution concerning claims that the ruins of old temples and other artifacts found in Mexico and Central America are positive evidence of the claims of *The Book of Mormon*.

The problem has become a sticky one for Mormon scholars who would like to be investigators in depth but are forbidden by their church authorities. Scores of books and pamphlets have been written by authorized writers for Mormon consumption and to be used for propaganda purposes. Mormons believe these writings because of their source. To tell a Mormon that *The Book of Mormon* has been proved by many archaeological evidences is very reassuring.

A very common claim made in Mormon propaganda is that the Smithsonian Institution used *The Book of Mormon* as a guide for research. According to a paper circulated among members of the Mormon church in Cleveland, Ohio, in 1959,

> The Book of Mormon was first brought to the attention of the Smithsonian Institution by James H. Fairchilds, a New York editor. At first the account was not taken seriously . . . It was recognized because it contained many excellent philosophical assertions, but

apparently was not regarded as having any historical
value until about 1884. . . . it was 1920 before the
Smithsonian Institute officially recognized the Book
of Mormon as a record of any value. All discoveries up
to this time were found to fit the Book of Mormon
accounts and so the heads of the Archaeological Department decided to make an effort to discover some
of the larger cities described in the Book of Mormon
records.

All members of the department were required to
study the account and make rough-maps of the various populated centers. When I visited the Smithsonian Institute Library in 1933 I noticed that there were
over thirty copies of the Book of Mormon on file.
During the past fifteen years the Institute has made
remarkable study of its investigations of the Mexican
Indians and it is true that the Book of Mormon has
been the guide to almost all of the major discoveries.

When Col. Lindbergh flew to South America five
years ago, he was able to sight heretofore undiscov-
ered cities which the archaeologists at the Institute
had mapped out according to the locations described
in the Book of Mormon. This record is now quoted by
the members of the Institute as an authority and is
recognized by all advanced students in the field.[2]

This completely false statement has been quoted to
this writer endlessly, and the Utah church has done
nothing to correct the statement. Teachers of the
young missionaries have done nothing to correct the
false impression, and these guileless young men seem
still to believe it and pass the message on to their
contacts, who have no way of knowing the facts or
rebutting the assertion.

The Smithsonian Institution has been so bothered

---

2. Jerald and Sandra Tanner, *Mormonism, Shadow or Reality*, p.
97.

by inquirers, both Mormon and non-Mormon, that
they have made a public and official rebuttal of the
idea. Dr. Frank H. H. Roberts, Jr., in a reply to an
inquiry by Arthur Budvarsen of La Mesa, California,
states:

> Permit me to say that the mistaken idea that the
> Book of Mormon has been used by scientific organiza-
> tions in conducting archaeological explorations has
> become quite current in recent years. It can be stated
> definitely that there is no connection between the
> archaeology of the New World and the subject matter
> of the Book of Mormon.
>
> There is no correspondence whatever between ar-
> chaeological sites and cultures as revealed by scien-
> tific investigations and as recorded in the Book of
> Mormon, hence the book cannot be regarded as hav-
> ing any historical value from the standpoint of the
> aboriginal peoples of the New World.
>
> The Smithsonian Institution has never officially
> recognized the Book of Mormon as a record of value
> on scientific matters, and the Book has never been
> used as a guide or source of information for discover-
> ing ruined cities.[3]

Mormon scientists have only recently entered into
the fields of anthropology and archaeology, undoubtedly because research in these fields, as they relate to
the supposed *Book of Mormon* countries and cultures, was turning up evidence quite contrary to the
claims of the book. Too late, they discovered that the
claims of professional Mormon apologists were making the church appear unscholarly. Regarding the
claims of Mormon missionaries that *The Book of*

3. Ibid., p. 98.

Mormon was now proved by archaeological finds, one of their own archaeologists writes,

> The statement that the Book of Mormon has already been proved by archaeology is misleading. The truth of the matter is that we are only now beginning to see even the outlines of the archaeological time-periods which could compare with those of the Book of Mormon. How, then, can the matter have been settled once and for all? That such an idea could exist indicates the ignorance of many of our people with regard to what is going on in the historical and anthropological sciences. . . .
>
> As for the notion that the Book of Mormon has already been proved by archaeology, I must say with Shakespeare, 'Lay not that flattering unction to your soul!' (Hamlet III:4).[4]

The Reorganized Church of Latter-Day Saints has been even more vocal than the Utah Church in defense of *The Book of Mormon*. They have also been the most devoted to Joseph Smith's version of the Bible. A recent paper by one of their educators indicates that they are having problems with the credibility of *The Book of Mormon*. Professor Wayne Ham comments:

> Extravagent claims about ancient American archaeology supporting the *Book of Mormon* have been made. Toltec, Mayan and even Aztec ruins, all of a comparatively late period, have been unfortunately identified with *Book of Mormon* peoples. Indian vocabulary lists have been compiled in an attempt to show a relationship between Indian languages and Hebrew and/or Egyptian. Brigham Young University

---

4. Ibid., pp. 98-99.

sponsored archaeological exploration near the Isthmus of Tehuantepec for several years in hopes of turning up some evidence to show that this area is the "narrow neck of land" mentioned in the *Book of Mormon,* all to no avail. To my knowledge, no non-Latter-day Saint archaeologist allows the *Book of Mormon* any place whatsoever in his reconstruction of the early history of the New World. Meanwhile, Mormon archaeologists and anthropologists are finding it prudent to become increasingly more cautious about admitting *Book of Mormon* data to their professional understandings of ancient American history and culture.[5]

Ham comments on the various inconsistencies in *The Book of Mormon,* its literary blunders, its anachronisms, the use of biblical quotations taken from the King James Version, et cetera. Then he concludes,

None of the above problem areas "disprove" *The Book of Mormon.* They do, however, raise some questions about our traditional understandings concerning the book. Perhaps for some church members answers to the questions raised in this article would seem to be readily available. For others, however, quick and easy answers will not solve the dilemma. Perhaps the time has come in the church to recognize that some members want to openly espouse a nonliteral view of the *Book of Mormon* . . . freed from some of the traditional hangups involved with having to accept unquestioningly the historicity of the *Book of Mormon,* these members could then read the book as a product of the American frontier and honor it as an

5. Wayne Ham, "Problems in Interpreting the Book of Mormon as History," *Courage: A Journal of History, Thought and Action,* p. 17.

interesting artifact of the Restoration movement in the nineteenth century, perhaps thus "enjoying" this fascinating piece of literature for the very first time.[6]

---

6. Ibid., p. 21.

18

The Sects of Mormonism

The Mormon missionaries at your door will present themselves as elders of the *one* church today that has a living prophet, a legitimate priesthood, a true baptism administered by qualified persons, and a set of inspired scriptures that complement the Bible.

They will not tell you that there have been some sixty sects[1] that have split from the original organization since its founding in 1830. In fact, the young missionaries usually do not know and have not been told that such divisions have occurred. All of these splinter sects claim the same prophet, Joseph Smith, and all claim that *The Book of Mormon* is the word of God. There are twenty or more of these sects still in existence.

Many of the smaller sects of this group disintegrated with the death of their founders or when the enthusiasm of the moment of founding diminished. A few persisted into a second or third generation, and some merged with other groups.

In a majority of cases, the reason for the founding of each sect was the reception of a "revelation" or a "vision" that indicated that the parent church had

---

1. Kate B. Carter, *Our Pioneer Heritage*, pp. 325-92.

been deficient in carrying out the "will of the Lord,"
and a new beginning was needed. It must be remem-
bered that the whole basis of Mormonism is the
claimed visions and revelations received by its
founder, Joseph Smith. Several others claimed to
have visions during the early days of the movement,
but they were thoroughly squelched by a revelation,
supposedly given by the Lord, that proclaimed, "But,
behold, verily, verily, I say unto thee, no one shall be
appointed to receive commandments and revelations
in this church excepting my servant Joseph Smith,
Jun., for he receiveth them even as Moses."[2]

Joseph Smith made provision for a transfer of this
authority by including this exception in the revelation: "For I have given him the keys of the mysteries,
and the revelations which are sealed, until I shall
appoint unto them another in his stead."[3] It came to
be recognized that the successors to Smith would
hold the office of prophet as well as president of the
church.

Following the death of the prophet, the succeeding
presidents supposedly were qualified to receive revelations, but few of them did. Brigham Young ex-
perimented with the "gift," but his attempts seemed
not to emanate from the same supernatural source. So
he gave up and relied on his own good judgment and
hunches. The presidents and prophets of the past
several decades have been much more prone to receive their revelations from the spirit of Dow-Jones.

The smaller sects were headed by sincere (or am-

2. Joseph Smith, *Doctrine and Covenants*, 28:2.
3. Ibid., 28:7.

bitious) individuals who continued to receive visions and revelations to the effect that they were appointed by the Lord to (1) assume the mantle of Joseph Smith, (2) reform the church, which had become apostate under the hands of Brigham Young or others, or (3) reactivate the necessity for the establishment of Zion in Independence, Missouri, or other places. These places included western Kansas,[4] the delta of the Colorado and Gila rivers in Arizona,[5] Mexico,[6] or the Beaver Islands in Lake Michigan.[7]

Independence, Missouri, drew several of these sects because of Joseph Smith's prophecies that indicated that location. For example, one dated July, 1831, says,

> Thus saith the Lord your God, if you will receive wisdom here is wisdom. Behold, the place which is now called Independence is the center place; and a spot for the temple is lying westward, upon a lot which is not far from the court-house.[8]

Zion was to be established and the temple built "in this generation."[9]

Of the twenty sects still functioning, apart from the Salt Lake City church, only a few are significant enough to be treated in this book. Most of them do little proselyting but stay in existence for the sake of principle.

---

4. Carter, p. 351.
5. Ibid., p. 349.
6. Ibid., p. 385.
7. Ibid., p. 343.
8. Joseph Smith, *Doctrine and Covenants*, 57:3.
9. Ibid., 84:4.

THE CHURCH OF JESUS CHRIST OF LATTER-DAY SAINTS,
STRANGITE

This church is almost extinct but it is an interesting
example of the art of "vision-getting." James J. Strang
was an attorney, schoolteacher, lecturer, editor, and
postmaster. He joined the church in Nauvoo in Feb-
ruary, 1844, and soon started on a mission, ordered by
Joseph Smith, to explore for a new location for the
church. He chose to explore in Wisconsin and, like
many others, had ambitions.

> On the same day that Joseph Smith and his brother
> Hyrum were martyred, according to Strang's later
> claim, an angel of the Lord appeared to him and told
> him to "fear God and be strengthened and obey him
> for great is the work, which he hath required at thy
> hands." The angel then "stretched forth his hand
> unto him and touched his head and put oil upon
> him."[10]

Strang claimed that he was in possession of a letter
dated June, 1844, in which the prophet told him that
he, Strang, was to be Smith's successor and president
of the church. The letter supposedly indicated Wisconsin as the new gathering place of the saints.

Besides gathering in the saints that lived in the
Wisconsin area, Strang gained a group of rather significant followers, including William Smith, brother
of the prophet; John E. Page, one of the former "twelve
apostles"; William E. Marks, former president of the
Nauvoo Stake; the entire Smith family (with the exception of Emma, Joseph's widow, and her minor
children); and a notorious character of Nauvoo days,

10. Carter, p. 342.

John C. Bennett, who was a strong supporter of Smith's plural-wife doctrine.

Strang was promptly ousted from the Nauvoo church by the twelve apostles. He did not get a chance to present the letter with his claims, and no one seems to have seen it, although a page of the postmaster's register in Nauvoo was cut out of the book and never located.

The followers of Strang accept *The Book of Mormon* and *The Doctrine and Covenants*, and Strang wrote a volume of scriptures of his own, *The Law of the Lord*, which he received in a vision.

Strang and his followers, numbering three thousand at one time, moved to the Beaver Islands in the northern part of Lake Michigan and established themselves as the Kingdom of St. James. Strang, of course, was anointed King James.

He advocated and practiced polygamy. This led to dissention. The king was assassinated by dissident members who were hiding in a woodpile. All five of his wives were pregnant at the time of his death. The church now has only a few followers.

THE CHURCH OF JESUS CHRIST, BICKERTONITE[11]

Bickerton was a follower of Sidney Rigdon after Rigdon's violent ejection from the church during the Missouri days. Rigdon and Oliver Cowdery were told to leave the area before daylight, under the threat of violence by the Danite avengers. They left. Rigdon went to Pennsylvania and attempted to start a new church.

Bickerton, who joined Rigdon's church in Pennsylvania, started to investigate the Salt Lake church and

11. Ibid., p. 350.

allied himself with one of its branches in West Elizabeth, Pennsylvania. He then left the Utah church over the problem of polygamy.

In 1874, as a result of a "revelation," the church was moved to St. John, Kansas. Bickerton was disfellowshipped in 1880, on the charge of adultery, and was succeeded by William Cadman. The present president is William H. Cadman.

The Bickertonite church has maintained something of a missionary outreach, including a mission to the Apache Indians at San Carlos, Arizona. A group in Africa joined the movement. Four splits have occurred in this church.

THE CHURCH OF CHRIST, HEDRICKITE

This church is located in Independence, Missouri. The distinctive claim of the Hedrickite church is that it is in possession of the piece of real estate that was set aside as the site of the Temple of Zion.

A pamphlet of the Temple Lot Church says,

> August 3, 1831, eight elders, viz., Joseph Smith, Jr., Oliver Cowdery, Sidney Rigdon, Peter Witmer, Jr., Frederick G. Williams, William W. Phelps, Martin Harris, and Joseph Coe, assembled together where the temple is to be erected. Sidney Rigdon dedicated the ground where the city is to stand; and Joseph Smith, Jr., laid a stone at the northeast corner of the contemplated temple in the name of the Lord Jesus of Nazareth. After all present had rendered thanks to the great ruler of the universe, Sidney Rigdon pronounced the spot of ground wholly dedicated unto the Lord forever. Amen.[12]

12. Charles L. Wheaton, *Historical Facts Concerning the Temple Lot*, p. 1.

The Temple Lot Church is located across the square from the tabernacle of the Reorganized Church of Jesus Christ of Latter-Day Saints and proudly displays the stone bearing the initials of Joseph Smith and the date 1831. Both the Reorganized Church and the Utah Church have sought to gain possession of the lot, by both purchase and litigation, but the Temple Lot is not for sale, and the property has been adjudicated as belonging to the present owners.

CHURCH OF CHRIST, FETTINGITE

Otto Fetting was ordained an apostle of the Temple Lot Church in 1926. At that time, there was a revival of interest in the building of the Temple of Zion. There was also a degree of cooperation between the Temple Lot and the Reorganized Church, each recognizing the priesthood of the other.

Fetting came prominently into the picture when he claimed to have had a two hour conference with John the Baptist at his home in Port Huron, Michigan, on November 30, 1930. Messages from the Baptist, through Fetting, continued to come, emphasizing the building of the temple and the establishment of Zion.

Fetting was more or less out of favor with the church in Independence, so his messages were despised; but they have continued to be circulated. A missionary circulating Fetting's revelations called on this writer recently.

THE FUNDAMENTALISTS

If you are a polygamist in Utah or the West, you are a Fundamentalist. At least thirteen separate groups, loosely knit, are identifiable.

Wilford Woodruff, president of the Utah church in 1890, issued what has become known as the Manifesto, supposedly terminating the practice of polygamy. This document is listed in the final pages of *The Doctrine and Covenants* as an OFFICIAL DECLARATION and addressed "To whom it may concern."

Utah was denied statehood because of its persistence in the practice of polygamy, and the federal government threatened heavy penalties unless the practice was officially discontinued.

After much pressure, Woodruff capitulated and prepared the carefully worded Manifesto. Scrutiny of the wording of the declaration shows that it says nothing about the wrongness of the principle of plural marriage; it merely denies that the church was presently teaching or encouraging its practice.

In the Manifesto, Woodruff, referring to the laws enacted against polygamy by the federal government, says, "I hereby declare my intention to submit to those laws, and to use my influence with the members of the Church over which I preside to have them do likewise." As a closing declaration, he adds, "I now publicly declare that my advice to the Latter-day Saints is to refrain from contracting any marriage forbidden by the law of the land."

It is noteworthy that the Manifesto does nothing to condemn the practice of plural marriage or to rescind section 132 of *The Doctrine and Covenants*, which demands plural marriage and sealing of marriages for eternity. It also states that no one will achieve the highest orders in the next life unless he takes a plurality of wives, sealed to him in the temple.

The Manifesto is not listed as a revelation by the

prophet and is printed in the back of *The Doctrine and Covenants* in a different format and type face than the 136 sections of the volume. It is not given as the word of the Lord and is not addressed to the saints but, rather, to the outside world. It had the result of easing government pressure, and statehood followed.

The document caused great embarrassment to many of the saints, especially the officials in the higher echelons who were the worst offenders. Many protested vigorously that the Manifesto violated the word of the Lord, as given in section 132, by Joseph Smith, and many refused to submit. Plural marriages were entered into for years afterward, even by presidents of the church, but solemnized outside of the territory, thus escaping the thrust of the Manifesto. Many marriages to plural wives were solemnized in Mexico. Probably many others were celebrated secretly and not recorded in public records. To the faithful, these were as binding as those celebrated legally.

The fundamentalist movement developed out of this strife and did not constitute the organization of a new church, because these adherents to the old cause considered themselves to be the orthodox section of the Utah church. They still consider themselves such.

The Salt Lake church has a policy of excommunicating any polygamous members if they are known or if they cause embarrassment to the main body. Most members of the main church today express themselves as out of sympathy with plural marriage, but in any prolonged conversation with them, one will find them defending the principle.

The fundamentalists, as a whole, belong to families

that were prominent in the church during the nineteenth century and include such families as Taylors, Cannons, Richards, Wooley, and Clawson. Areas where polygamy is presently being practiced include a section of Salt Lake City; Bountiful, Utah; southern Utah at the Arizona border; northern Arizona; southeastern Arizona; and Mexico. It has been estimated that there are some thirty thousand people in Utah involved in polygamous families.

The Reorganized Church of Jesus Christ of Latter-Day Saints, which is the second largest sect, will be discussed in a separate chapter.

19

The Reorganized Church of Jesus Christ of Latter-Day Saints

When Joseph Smith and his brother Hyrum were assassinated in the Carthage jail on June 27, 1844, the entire political, social, and religious system was in a state of near chaos. Three distinct factions were in a state of ferment. Joseph Smith was the focus of the entire problem.

Within the church were two factions. The group surrounding the prophet and his twelve apostles was busy making money, and Joseph was running for president and parading as lieutenant general of the Nauvoo Legion. The revelation on plural marriage was being formulated, with Smith and his cronies denying it vehemently.

Also inside the church was a conservative group consisting of those who opposed the plural marriage idea and seemed quite aware that the doctrine was being practiced. Some had already become apostate but were still living in Nauvoo and trying to correct affairs by undermining the prophet and his ambitions.

Outside the establishment, and outside of Nauvoo,
were those who feared the prophet's political preten-
sions and were confident that they were being
exploited by the saints and that the robberies and
murders that were occurring were being perpetrated
by an element living in Nauvoo and using the infamous city charter as a protection against prosecution.

Both the dissident within the city of Nauvoo and
the church, and the apprehensive group outside of the
establishment, believed that there was no hope of
relief as long as the prophet was alive. And there was
little hope of his being deposed from high office. So
assassination was in the air.

The crisis came when the dissident group within
the city started a newspaper, *The Expositor*, and in
their first and only issue exposed the new revelation
on polygamy and published affidavits of various mis-
doings of the inner circle of Mormonism. The document, looked at today, seems quite moderate in tone
but at the time would certainly have seemed quite
inflammatory. Smith immediately called the city
council together, had the newspaper declared a nui-
sance, ordered the press destroyed, and ordered all
copies of the paper confiscated. This was done, which
made Smith vulnerable to arrest. That was the event
that led directly to the assassination of the prophet.

Instead of destroying the Mormon establishment,
the murder of Smith provided the church with a martyr and assured its continuation. There was a scram-
ble for the office of president to succeed Joseph Smith.
If the prophet had lived, young Joseph, twelve years
old at the time, would have succeeded his father, but

the situation was too critical for even a regent to handle.

Sidney Rigdon, who was Smith's theologian, was quickly excluded by the Twelve. Cowdery had already been excommunicated. David Whitmer, one of the witnesses to *The Book of Mormon*, was out of favor with the leaders. Alpheus Cutler and James J. Strang each received visions to the effect that they were ordered by the Lord to succeed the prophet. Each acquired a following.

Brigham Young, who did not rely on visions, went to work promoting enough support to have himself elected as president. The majority followed Young. He immediately started to make plans for an exodus to the West.

Emma Smith, Joseph's widow, followed no one but retired east with her four sons. She later married Major Bidamon and to all appearances desired to leave the Mormon system behind. However, she carried with her some token of the prophet's office, including the manuscript of Joseph's *Inspired Version* of the Bible.

James Strang garnered the greatest number of the group that did not follow Brigham Young. He established the new church in Wisconsin and eventually set up the Kingdom of St. James on the Beaver Islands of northern Lake Michigan. Polygamy was introduced in Strang's church, and irritations followed. Strang was assassinated in June, 1856, and his church started to disintegrate.

Meanwhile, Joseph III was growing up, and a number of those who had followed Strang and Brigham Young felt that it was time to reorganize the

church with young Joseph as its president. Joseph
was not the least bit interested at first but eventually
submitted.

The new church was begun in 1859 and soon had its
headquarters in Independence, Missouri, where
Joseph the prophet had declared, by revelation, Zion
was to be built. Jason Briggs had followed Strang and
then left Strang and followed the prophet's brother,
William. He promoted young Joseph and, with Zenes
Gurley, established a new presidency. The term
"Josephite" has been used to describe the Reorganized Church. They followed the decision that the
presidency of the new church should descend in the
line of the original prophet.

The distinctives of the new church included a firm
stand on rejecting the doctrine of polygamy, rejecting
all of the writings of Brigham Young, and rejecting
those writings that they believed were written by
Young but attributed to Joseph Smith.

They accept *The Doctrine and Covenants* that were
written before Smith's death, and, of course, reject
vehemently section 132 of *The Doctrine and Covenants* of the Utah church. They insist that this was the
work of Young, written after the death of the prophet,
and not announced until 1852. This, of course, cannot
be substantiated, because it was this revelation, exposed by the destroyed *Expositor*, that precipitated
the imprisonment and death of the prophet.

They reject the *King Follett Discourse*, which establishes fully the doctrine of God being an exalted man
and man being a potential god. This is certainly the
last public address of the prophet, but the Reorganized Church insists that it was either written or

revised to suit Brigham Young. This is highly improbable, as Brigham was too busy in the six weeks after the prophet's death to undertake such a chore of writing or revision.

The Reorganized Church does not accept *The Pearl of Great Price*, particularly the Book of Abraham, which establishes the ineligibility of Negroes to become priests. Certainly the whole of *The Pearl of Great Price* was written by Smith.

The Book of Mormon is accepted as being the word of God, whereas they say that the Bible *contains* the word of God. They accept Joseph Smith's *Inspired Version*, which is certainly a distortion of the King James Version, with additions and changes where the King James Version did not agree with Smith's doctrine.

The Reorganized Church does not practice baptism for the dead, does not have the elaborate priesthoods that the Utah Church has, and does not have the temple initiatory rites.

20

Mormon Buildings

Christians are sometimes confused in their terminology when describing edifices erected by the Mormons. Someone will report that a new Mormon temple is being erected in his neighborhood. These buildings, being finished at the rate of at least one a day, are not temples but ward chapels. They are the equivalent of the churches of the various denominations and serve the local membership as a meeting place. The buildings are equipped with chapel, social and dance hall, and general facilities for various types of occasions.

Temples, of which there are less than twenty, are the buildings where esoteric rites are conducted. They can be entered only by those who have paid their tithes, have a "recommend" from their bishop, and have work to do for the dead.

Tabernacles are erected in a few places, the best known being on the temple grounds in Salt Lake City, Utah. This has become something of a tourist attraction as well as being an auditorium for general assembly of the members of the church.

At certain places in the mountainous West, one will

see warehouses, grain storage silos, and so on, with the title "Bishop's Storehouse." These are facilities for storing and processing the tithes-in-kind of the faithful and are purely business facilities for the church.

Church buildings of the smaller sects of Mormonism, such as the Church of Christ, Temple Lot, the Reorganized Church of Jesus Christ of Latter-Day Saints, and the Church of Jesus Christ, Bickertonite, are of the more conventional type. The fundamentalists (polygamous Utah Mormons) do not usually meet in distinctive buildings.

Mormon temples are distributed throughout the world in some fifteen or more strategic locations. The first temple was built in Kirtland, Ohio, before the present elaborate temple rites were developed. It served the purpose of a conventional church building as well as having secret chambers for ritual purposes. It still stands and is owned by the Reorganized Church of Jesus Christ of Latter-Day Saints, whose headquarters are in Independence, Missouri.

A temple, in fact *the* temple of a restored Zion, was projected and a cornerstone laid in Independence, where Joseph Smith prophesied the final temple would be. Jesus Christ would set up His Kingdom there, and all the nations would flow to it. Smith repeatedly prophesied that the temple would be built in his generation. Unfortunately the gentile pioneers, who were already settled there, decided against the saints and their militant kingdom. The state militia clashed with Smith's "army of Israel." The Missourians won, and the saints left, licking their wounds and crying, "Persecution" and "Massacre." The

prophecy of Joseph Smith, that Zion would be established in Independence, was dramatically canceled.

Smith was murdered within a few years and those
who survived him kept wondering, throughout their
lifetimes, when the prophecy would be fulfilled. A
century and a half later, the saints are still wondering
but are sure that someday Zion in Missouri will be
realized.

Nauvoo, Illinois, on the banks of the Mississippi,
became the next temple location. The elaborate
Nauvoo temple was not yet finished in 1844, when
Joseph Smith and his brother Hyram were murdered.
The building was hastily completed to a point where
endowment rites could be administered, just before
the Mormons were again expelled. The largest seg-
ment of the church followed Brigham Young to Utah.
Nauvoo was abandoned, and the temple destroyed.

The present temple, in Salt Lake City, on the pinna-
cle of which the angel Moroni stands blowing his
trumpet, was commenced in 1853, but was not for-
mally dedicated until 1893. It was used, of course, for
all its intended purposes before the dedication date. A
smaller temple annex has recently been built because
of the increased demands for the performance of temple rites. Other temples have been built throughout
the United States, Canada, Europe, and the South
Pacific. The latest has now been completed in the
environs of Washington, D.C., and is the most impos-
ing building on the Washington skyline. It is an ar-
chitectural monstrosity.

Temple buildings, of which the Mormons boast,
and the secret rites for which these temples are built
are the evidence of a deep-rooted paganism in the

philosophy of salvation of the Mormon system. The Reorganized Church of Jesus Christ of Latter-Day Saints and other branches of the church do not build temples and do not have the systems of ritual of the Salt Lake church.

In a pamphlet entitled *Why Mormons Build Temples*, Mark E. Peterson, a member of the Council of the Twelve Apostles of the Utah church, defends the system of temple building and the performance of rituals. In the first two pages of the booklet, he makes the following statements:

(1). In Biblical times sacred ordinances were administered in holy edifices for the spiritual salvation of ancient Israel . . . they were specially constructed for this particular purpose.

(2). While the people travelled in the wilderness, they used a portable tabernacle. This tabernacle was called "the temple of the Lord."

(3). Following the pattern of Biblical days, the Lord again in our day has provided these ordinances for the salvation of all who will believe, and directs that temples be built in which to perform these sacred rites.

(4). Anciently, to obtain the saving blessings of the Lord, it was necessary for an individual to do two things: 1) live the righteous life prescribed in the commandments of the Lord, and 2) participate in the saving ordinances administered by the Lord's truly authorized servants.

(5). Although some of these ordinances could be performed wherever the people found themselves, others were so sacred that the Lord required that they be performed in a specially built edifice, such as the Tabernacle or Temple, as at first, or the great Temple which replaced it.

(6). There the priesthood ministered in solemn rites. Not everyone could enter, only those of proven worthiness.

(7). The holy ordinances were never fully made known to the world at large; they were too sacred, but the chosen and faithful participated in all solemnity.[1]

All of the above statements are either untrue or grossly misleading. One would wonder how a man who professes to be an apostle could be so ignorant of the text of Scripture as to make the above statements. Either he is ignorant and unread, or he is deliberately intending to mislead his readers into accepting his premise that the modern Mormon rituals are a restoration of the ancient rituals of Israel and that the Mormon temples are the restored counterpart of the Temple of God in Jerusalem in biblical times.

Since Peterson's argument is vital to the proper understanding of what Mormonism really is, we propose to challenge Peterson's points and demonstrate that Mormonism and its temples and rites are not Israelitish, biblical, or Christian, but totally pagan.

Peterson's first point is partly true: there was a portable tabernacle used in the wilderness while the Israelites were journeying to the promised land. It was used until the first Temple, Solomon's, was built. The Temple built by Solomon was restored following the captivity, and Herod's Temple was built on the same site and was in use while our Lord was on earth. No regional temples have ever been built because Jerusalem was specified as the one place Jehovah would meet with His people. There was only one Temple in Israel.

1. Mark E. Peterson, *Why Mormons Build Temples*, p. 3.

Concerning point number two: the tabernacle was never called the "temple of the Lord."

Concerning point number three: the Mormon temples do not follow the pattern of biblical days. The only physical resemblance between them and the Temple in Jerusalem is the laver, which rests on the backs of twelve oxen. The Mormons have made this into a baptismal font. It was never used for that purpose in the Temple of Jehovah.

In this section, Peterson also establishes his premise that the temple is a place for the administration of "ordinances for the salvation of all who will believe" and vindicates the Mormon activity of building temples.

The only ordinances performed in the Temple in Jerusalem were the offering of sacrifices for the sins of the people and the offering of worship by the priests for the whole people of Israel. Mormons have no such ordinances. No such ordinances existed in the apostolic Church. The two recognized ordinances of evangelical Christian churches are baptism and the Lord's Supper, and these are for those who are already children of God.

In point four, Peterson is simply proposing two facets of Mormon teaching that are foreign to Christian doctrine. He is saying that salvations acquired by living a righteous life and participating in the ordinances. This is far from the methodology of salvation in ancient Israel and in the Christian Church. God recognized that no one could live a righteous life: this was demonstrated by the fact that men could not fulfill the requirements of the Mosaic Law. Ordi-

nances in Israel were for the atonement of the sins of
the people and consisted of offering blood sacrifices
in recognition of the fact that the suppliant was under
the sentence of death because of his sins.

Individual salvation of an Israelite was accomplished only when he, as a suppliant, brought the
prescribed sacrifice to be offered by the priest. National salvation was invoked in the annual offering on
the Day of Atonement, when the high priest, alone,
entered the Holy of Holies with the blood of the sacrifice, "which he offered for himself, and for . . . the
people" (Hebrews 9:7). All Israel was recognized as
being under the blood, from the smallest babe to the
oldest patriarch and from the saint to the miscreant.

The Christian emphasis is that the sacrifices offered
on the various occasions in Old Testament times were
types of the one great Sacrifice that would be offered
by the Lamb of God on Calvary. Both the priest and the
multitude recognized that they were sinners in the
offering of the sacrifices, and Christians today recognize that only by a personal acceptance of the merits
of Calvary are sins put away.

Mormons teach that Jesus died for Adam's transgression, and that we, being thus immunized from
Adam's transgression, must make amends for our
own sins. They teach that we are not born sinners, but
that we become sinners. Our own efforts are required
to take care of current transgressions. *The Book of
Mormon* expresses the process: "We are saved by the
grace of Christ after all that we can do."[2]

In points five and six, Peterson says that the ordinances were administered in solemn rites, in the sa-

2. Joseph Smith, *Book of Mormon*, 2 Nephi 25:23.

cred precincts, and that "only those of proved worthiness" could enter these precincts. This, of course, is
not true. The sacrifices were administered only by the
high priest and his assistants, who were required to be
the lineal descendants of Aaron, the first high priest.
Other Temple duties were performed by members of
the tribe of Levi. (Joseph Smith claimed to be a
spiritual descendant of Ephraim, which would disqualify him as a priest. Only descendants of Levi
could become priests.) Sad to relate, many unworthy
persons, such as the sons of Eli, officiated in the
priestly offices of Israel.

Peterson's final statement shows the grossest ignorance of the sacred Scriptures. Nothing was hidden
or secret from the populace at large. Every Israelite
knew what was going on when the priests officiated;
many long chapters of the Old Testament are devoted
to the intricate details of all of the procedures in the
sacred precincts. The "chosen and faithful" ministers, as we have stated, were the hereditary priests and
Levites whose qualifications and endowments are
clearly defined. Nothing was secret. Even the activities of the Day of Atonement were well known to
every Israelite, and the Law demanded that they be
explained in every generation and household.

In complete contrast to the ritualism of ancient
Israel, the Mormon temples are devoted to two principal ordinances. One is the baptisms for the dead, by
which persons who were not able to get to the temples, or deceased relatives and ancestors who knew
nothing of Mormonism, can be brought into the benefits of the Mormon plan in the resurrection. The
other principal ritual is that of celestial marriage, in

which couples are sealed for eternity as mates, and proxy marriages for those who are unable to get to one of the temples. Both concepts are quite unscriptural and definitely pagan in concept.

The Mormon theologians have never discovered that when Christ died on Calvary, as the one Sacrifice that could put away sin, the Temple services and their symbolism were forever fulfilled and terminated.

The believer in the Lord Jesus has full access into the presence of God. "There is . . . one mediator between God and men, the man Christ Jesus" (1 Timothy 2:5). All believers are holy priests, offering up spiritual sacrifices (1 Peter 2:5), and royal priests (1 Peter 2:9), by reason of the new birth and not by the benefit of any human ordination or laying on of hands. Neither the apostolic Church nor the Christian Scriptures know anything of priesthoods or rites such as those of the Mormons.

21

Persecuted Saints

The Mormons have been able, through the years, to maintain an image of a body of saints persecuted for their faith. After untold hardships, they were forced out of their homes and communities to seek sanctuary in the far West, where they could worship as they chose.

They tell of persecution by the scoffers and hoodlums of New York State and the "mobocrats" of Missouri and Illinois. Dramatic romance has been built around their migration to the valley of the Salt Lake, fleeing from the wrath of the gentiles, pushing handcarts containing all their worldly goods.

Even after their arrival and settlement in the mountains of Utah, they tell of their persecutors following them. Every criticism leveled against them has been heralded as religious persecution.

Every objective student of history knows that Americans have not persecuted religious minorities because of their beliefs, strange as they may be. We have questioned their sanity, laughed at their antics, and expressed our criticism of their beliefs in explosive terms. We have written books about them. But we have not "mobbed" them or exiled them.

Literally scores of books have been written criticizing the Mormons, and scores of denials and rebuttals have been produced by them in return. This is not persecution. This is healthy dialogue.

True, the Mormons left New York State for Ohio in the early 1830s, but this was largely because their New York neighbors could not see them as saints and prophets. The "hoodlums" of the area were not persecutors, but simply Joseph Smith's old gang of treasure hunters, who felt that Joseph was "holding out" on them with his treasure of golden plates. The attraction in Ohio was Sidney Rigdon's ready-made congregation, which moved into the Mormon church as a body.

They left Kirtland, with its newly built temple, largely because of the shady banking and real estate operations of Smith and Rigdon. Many had apostatized by that time. Those who hastened the exodus westward were not gentile persecutors, but dissident Mormons who had attached themselves to the church and then, disillusioned, sought revenge against the leaders. The rank and file of honest folk who followed westward did so in good faith.

Their expulsion from Missouri and Illinois, likewise, was not because of their religious beliefs but because of their behavior. In both cases, they had become undesirable neighbors.

The present writer has always avoided writing about this phase of Mormonism, but since this book is about Mormon methods and beliefs, it must be dealt with. The problem is that Mormon missionaries are still using this persecution complex as an argument against their critics. In 1973, a correspondent in New Zealand wrote,

> Please explain to me the motivation behind why it
> was that Baptist, Methodist, and Presbyterian minis-
> ters who organized and led mobs who tarred and
> feathered Joseph Smith, broke one of his teeth while
> trying to force him to drink poison; then stood idly by
> while his followers were murdered, their homes
> burned, women raped; and did nothing to stop their
> good church people from murdering Joseph Smith?[1]

Obviously our correspondent in New Zealand, who
admits knowing little about the times and back-
grounds of the Mormon story, got this recital from
Mormon missionaries, who, in turn, were taught such
propaganda by their superiors before going on their
mission.

We question the integrity of any teacher of young
missionaries in Salt Lake who would condense into
one gross paragraph such a collection of unrelated
untruths and half-truths and plant them in the minds
of young missionaries going to the other side of the
world to propagandize their church.

Does our correspondent in New Zealand think that
these Baptist, Methodist, and Presbyterian ministers
traveled from Kirtland, Ohio, six hundred miles to
western Missouri, and then, several years later, four
hundred miles back to Nauvoo, Illinois, just to gloat
over women being raped and houses burned?

What are the facts? Joseph Smith and his mother,
Lucy, identify the persons who tarred and feathered
the prophet and Sidney Rigdon. Rigdon was a prime
target, as well as Smith. There was not a Presbyterian,
Methodist, or Baptist among them. Joseph Smith says
that there were about a dozen men, including

---

1. Personal correspondence. Letter to the author, March 10, 1973.

Simonds Rider, a Campbellite preacher, and Peletiah
Allen, Esq. He also mentions three sons of Father
Johnson, with whom Joseph was lodging, as being
apostates from Mormonism.[2]

Faun Brodie also mentions Ezra Booth and adds the
detail that Eli Johnson, one of the sons of Father
Johnson, demanded that the prophet be castrated because he suspected that Smith had been intimate with
Eli's sister, Nancy Maranda.[3] This all happened near
Hiram, Ohio, on March 24, 1832. The entire tarring
and feathering band was apparently made up of disaf-
fected Mormons, who before had been Campbellites,
and then, in turn, members of Rigdon's church. Certainly they all knew Rigdon.

The whole story of the Kirtland period is one of
politics, a rabble society, a radical church with visions, tongues, spells, visitations of angels, charges
and denials of polygamy, and, finally, real estate and
banking wheeling and dealing that ended in bank-
rupting the community as well as the never solvent
bank. Smith and Rigdon left Kirtland on horseback
between dark and dawn and did not rest until they
were two hundred miles away, fearing their pursuers.

Bear in mind that this is not gentile propaganda.
The church was in disorder and bankrupt, and
Joseph, in disrepute, even with his most devoted
former followers. Joseph himself said,

> At this time the spirit of speculation in lands and
> property of all kinds . . . was taking root in the church.

2. Lucy Mack Smith, *Biographical Sketches of Joseph Smith the
   Prophet and His Progenitors for Many Generations*, p. 194.
3. Fawn M. Brodie, *No Man Knows My History: The Life of Joseph
   Smith, the Mormon Prophet*, p. 119.

As the fruits of this spirit, evil surmisings, fault finding, disunion, dissention, and apostasy followed in quick succession, and it seemed as though all the powers of earth and hell were combining their influence . . . to overthrow the church at once.[4]

One might infer from this that Smith was recording the sins of the members in general, but excluding himself. As a matter of fact, he was one of the most acquisitive landholders of the church and owned the most valuable holdings, purchasing them at low prices and selling them for many times their cost.

Apostle Parley P. Pratt, probably one of Smith's most loyal supporters, wrote the prophet,

Having long pondered the path in which we as a people, have been led in regard to our temporal management, I have at length become fully convinced that the whole scheme of speculation in which we have been engaged, is of the devil. I allude to the covetous, extortionary speculating spirit which has reigned in this place for the last season; which has given rise to lying, deceiving and taking advantage of one's neighbor, and in short, every evil work.

And being as fully convinced that you, and President Rigdon, both by precept and example, have been the principle means in leading this people astray, in these particulars, and having myself been led astray and caught in the same snare by your example, and by false prophesying and preaching, from your own mouths, yea, having done many things wrong and plunged myself and family, and others, well nigh into destruction, I have awoke to an awful sense of my situation. . . .

4. B. H. Roberts, *A Comprehensive History of the Church of Jesus Christ of Latter-Day Saints,* 2:487-88.

> And now dear brother, if you are still determined to
> pursue this wicked course, until yourself and the
> church shall sink down to hell. . . .[5]

The most flagrant fraud, and the one that caused the
hasty exit of Smith and Rigdon to escape their pursuers, was their venture into the banking business.
The bank was denied a charter but was started any-
way. It was illegally operated and dishonestly administered. It issued $250,000 worth of bills, which
were backed by no assets. Many besides Mormons
invested and deposited in it to their sorrow. The out-
siders added to the friction, causing the flight of
Smith and Rigdon and the collapse of the whole Kirtland enterprise. None of this, however, was religious
persecution by the gentiles.

At the time of the Kirtland debacle, Heber Kimball,
one of Smith and Brigham Young's closest associates,
said, "There were not twenty people on earth that
would declare that Joseph Smith was a prophet of
God."[6]

Charles Kelly and Hoffman Birney, in their biog-
raphy of Porter Rockwell, one of the Danites, sum up
the Mormon claim of persecution.

> They have ever been swaggering, quarrelsome and
> challenging; tactless to the point of downright stupid-
> ity. Religion itself, doctrinal differences between
> Mormonism and the more orthodox faiths, has had
> little or nothing to do with the persecution which the
> saints assert has ever been their lot. The expulsion

5. Jerald and Sandra Tanner, *Mormonism, Shadow or Reality*, p.
   529.
6. Gary Dean Guthrie, "Joseph Smith as an Administrator," pp.
   85-86.

from Missouri, the death of the Prophet and the downfall of Nauvoo, the enforced migration to the Great Basin, were occasioned only by Mormon belligerency, defiance of law and custom, and the fundamental conviction entertained by every Latter-day Saint that to rob or cheat a Gentile was to perform a holy deed.

Persecution has ever been the Mormon battle cry, but Joseph the Prophet and Hyrum the Patriarch might have lived to die peacefully in bed had they not so heartily encouraged the robbing of Gentile hen roosts, the stealing of cattle and horses, the pillaging of lonely homesteads. Their old age might have been truly patriarchal if Nauvoo had not been made the headquarters for the manufacture of counterfeit money and a haven for every bandit of the Mississippi River bottoms. That end would have been attained through the exercise of a quality which the Mormons, as a people, have never possessed—a tiny modicum of common sense.[7]

7. Charles Kelly and Hoffman Birney, *Holy Murder: The Story of Porter Rockwell*, pp. 37-38.

22

The Troubles in Missouri

One would think that the Mormons would be smart enough to cease talking about their troubles with the Missourians back in the 1830s, especially since they got their revenge on the gentiles, specifically the Missourians, when they massacred the 126 members of the Fancher Train at Mountain Meadows in southern Utah in 1856.

The massacre was planned and executed after much deliberation. After the perpetrators piously kneeled in prayer, with their shoulders touching, they arose to do the deed. It is considered one of the most cold-blooded massacres of whites by whites in the annals of America. The story of the Mountain Meadows affair has been told many times, by both Mormon and gentile writers. The episode cancels out any claims of the Mormons that Joseph Smith was a martyr and that his followers were a persecuted people. Martyrs do not take revenge and hold grudges.

Another in the roll of Mormon martyrs is Parley P. Pratt, who was shot and bludgeoned in Arkansas on April 13, 1857, for the exercise of his religious principles—he was shot from his horse while riding off with the seduced wife of Hector McLean. She would have been Pratt's twelfth wife. The enraged husband took exception with a shotgun. Pratt's biographer closes her book with the following quotation:

> Under no conditions can we excuse or condone the Mountain Meadows massacre, and yet to those assassins who rode away from that horrible field of slaughter, it seemed that Parley Pratt had been avenged.[1]

We insist that the troubles in Missouri were not persecutions by gentiles because of the Mormon religious beliefs. The clashes were not between religious and nonreligious opponents. The Mormons have never displayed any of the graces of religion in their migrations and settlements. In Missouri, their religion was of the sword and inflammatory speeches and not of the heart and life.

Their adversaries, the Missourians, were rough-and-tumble frontiersmen who fought their way west and settled their farms by brute strength. They did not profess to be religionists and were probably as rough a set of pioneers as the Mormons. The tactless Mormons publicly and loudly announced that they would drive the settlers out of the Lord's inheritance—by purchase, if convenient; by force, if necessary.

The action was armed force against armed force. Joseph Smith's army, the core of which was the now well-documented Danites, was a solid block both at the voting booth and in the field. The citizen force was a hastily raised volunteer militia. Scruples on both sides were thrown to the wind. What makes the

---

1. Reva Stanley, *Archer of Paradise*, p. 333.

Mormons so bitter about it all is that they lost the war. The citizens sent them packing without displaying any tenderness.

If the Mormons had moved into Missouri as ordinary pioneers, they would have been as acceptable as any band of settlers in the new frontier. There was plenty of room for all, and the Mormons had skills that would have been valued. The Missourians would not have cared if the Mormons worshiped Muhammad or Baal, as long as they behaved themselves as citizens and worked hard clearing their farms.

The Mormons made their big blunder by fanatically following the fantastic claim of Joseph Smith that they were destined to establish Zion and the kingdom of God in Missouri. Smith's whole structure of kingdom-building was based on an ignorance of scriptural interpretation and dependence on the radical thinking of Sidney Rigdon, who conjured up the idea that the church needed restoration. The Mormons claim to have restored it in 1830.

The kingdom was to have been established and the temple set up in "this generation," said Smith. The place, according to revelation, was Independence, Missouri. Smith selected a lot and set up a cornerstone on it, engraved with his initials and the date. He also prophesied that he would live until the Lord's coming. He was dead, by lynching, in 1844. The temple lot is now held by a splinter denomination of Mormonism, with no temple in sight.

23

The Expulsion from Illinois

In 1847, the Mormons were driven out of their city of Nauvoo, where they had concentrated their activities after being driven from Missouri. It was an ugly mess, and the Mormons have cried "persecution" ever since. Again, when the facts are known, it will be seen that the persecution was not because of the religious views of the saints but because of their behavior.

Edward Bonney's recently republished book, *The Banditti of the Prairies*, tells of the lawlessness of western Illinois in the days before the expulsion of the Mormons. While Bonney is something of a braggart, he does relate first person facts that are a matter of history in Illinois and cannot be ignored. Mormons, of course, say that it is all gentile lies. Until they read the book for themselves. Then they say nothing. Dr. Philip D. Jordan writes in the introduction,

> During the 1840's, counterfeiters, horse thieves, stage robbers and murderers plagued western Illinois and eastern Iowa. Singly, and in well organized bands, desperados disrupted the peace not only in the vicinity of Nauvoo but also in the trans-Mississippi towns of Port Madison, Burlington and Davenport in

Iowa Territory. Bonney believed that "in no case could the perpetrators of the crimes be arrested and brought to justice." Then he added: "In case of an arrest at Nauvoo the accused were immediately released by the city authorities, and the cry of "persecution against the saints" raised, effectively drowning out the pleas for justice of the injured and the officer forced to return and tell a tale of defeat. This done, the fugitive found a safe shelter under the wide spread wings of the Mormon leaders and laughed at pursuit.[1]

Bonney's experiences as a detective show that only if a criminal was apprehended while away from Nauvoo and brought to trial by a court not under the influence of the Mormons, could a conviction be gained. Even in such cases, the Mormons produced countless witnesses to testify in favor of the criminal.

Undoubtedly, there was a majority of the inhabitants of Nauvoo who were honest, law-abiding citizens. The facts of history show, however, that it was highly placed Mormons, aided and abetted by the peculiar and infamous city charter of Nauvoo, that flouted justice and brought the onus of guilt on the people as a whole. Counterfeiting was undoubtedly the grossest form of swindling perpetrated by the denizens of Nauvoo.

It is significant that eight of the Twelve Apostles, including Brigham Young, were under indictment for counterfeiting when they started their hasty exodus to Utah. It is also significant that the crime problem of that part of Illinois diminished notably when the Mormons left.

---

1. Philip D. Jordan, "Introduction," *The Banditti of the Prairies*, by Edward Bonney.

24

Summary

Joseph Smith went to his death with a smoking revolver in his hands. His followers swore vengeance on his killers to the third and fourth generation. They got their revenge many fold. Brigham Young, Joseph Smith's successor, slavishly followed the pattern of his mentor. His last audible words were, "Joseph—Joseph—Joseph."

The Lord Jesus went to the cross, not as the victim of a mob, but as a willing victim, the Lamb of God, taking away the sin of the world. As He died, He prayed for His murderers: "Father, forgive them; for they know not what they do" (Luke 23:34).

Stephen, the first disciple of the Lord Jesus to earn a martyr's crown, was beaten to death with cobblestones because of his testimony for his Saviour. His last words were, "Lord, lay not this sin to their charge" (Acts 7:60).

In the past nineteen hundred years, millions have gone to their deaths, not to gain merit or earn salvation, but because they would not compromise their testimony for the Lord Jesus.

Millions of others who were of the human refuse of this earth have been reclaimed and transformed by the grace of God and have gone on to serve the Lord in winning others, not to gain salvation by their good works, but because of their love for Christ.

We have been discussing doctrine—Christian doctrine versus Mormon doctrine. The line of cleavage between the two is very clear.

Christian doctrine proposes that man is a sinner by nature and by practice and can do nothing to pay for his sins. God alone can take care of the sin question, and this He did at Calvary. Salvation from sin, provided by Calvary, is made available to man on the basis of a gift of grace. The whole operation is based on the fact that God is the God of the Bible, and not a god who is an exalted human, made god by self-effort.

Mormon doctrine proposes that man is not inherently a sinner and can do enough good works to assure himself a place in the favor of a god who is like himself.

Experimentally, the Gospel of Jesus Christ gives a complete joy and assurance of everlasting life, here and now, and an incentive to perform good deeds out of love for the Saviour.

By their own testimony, Mormons are never sure if they have done enough ritualistic works to insure salvation. In fact, salvation is no more than a term to express cumulative self-improvement that, it is hoped, will terminate in exaltation at the time of death.

The choice of which road to follow is the choice of each individual. It is as simple as that.

Bibliography

THE WRITINGS OF JOSEPH SMITH, JR.

The Book of Mormon. Salt Lake Ed. Salt Lake City, 1961.

The Doctrine and Covenants of the Church of Jesus Christ of Latter-Day Saints. Salt Lake Ed. Salt Lake City: Deseret, 1921, 1973.

The Holy Scriptures. Known as the Inspired Version. Plano, Iowa: Reorganized Church of Jesus Christ of Latter-Day Saints, 1867.

King Follett Discourse. With notes and references by the late Elder B. H. Roberts of the First Council of Seventy. Salt Lake City: Magazine Printing Co., 1955.

"Lectures on Faith." Doctrine and Covenants, 1890 ed. Salt Lake City: Deseret, 1890.

The Pearl of Great Price. Salt Lake City: Church of Jesus Christ of Latter-Day Saints, 1954.

BOOKS, PAMPHLETS, AND PERIODICALS

Barker, James L. The Divine Church. A course of study for the Melchizedek Priesthood Quorums. Salt Lake City: Deseret, 1952.

Brodie, Fawn McKay. No Man Knows My History: The Life of Joseph Smith, the Mormon Prophet. New York: Knopf, 1945.

Carter, Kate B. Our Pioneer Heritage. Salt Lake City: Daughters of Utah Pioneers, 1962.

Chafer, Lewis Sperry. *Systematic Theology.* Dallas: Dallas Theo. Sem., 1947.

Christianson, Ross T. Articles in *University Archaeological Society News Letter,* no. 64, January 30, 1960.

Cowdery, Oliver. *Defense: In a Rehearsal of My Grounds for Separating Myself from the Latter-Day Saints.* Norton, Ohio: Pressley's Job Shop, 1839.

Curtis, Bardella Shipp. *Sacred Scriptures and Religious Philosophy.* Caldwell, Idaho: Caxton, 1922.

The Deseret News, January 16, 1952.

Ensign, April, May 1971.

Evans, John Henry. *An American Prophet.* New York: Macmillan, 1933.

Guthrie, Gary Dean. "Joseph Smith as an Administrator." Master's thesis, Brigham Young U., 1969.

Hackney, W. Gordon. *That Adam-God Doctrine.* Salt Lake City: privately printed, 1962.

Ham, Wayne. "Problems in Interpreting the Book of Mormon as History." *Courage: A Journal of History, Thought and Action* 1 (September 1970):15 ff.

Hanson, Paul M. *Jesus Christ Among the Early Americans.* Independence, Mo.: Herald, 1959.

Hastings, James, ed. *Dictionary of the Bible.* Rev. ed. New York: Scribner, 1963.

Hinckley, Gordon B. *What of the Mormons?* Salt Lake City: Church of Jesus Christ of Latter-Day Saints, 1947.

Hunter, Milton R. *The Gospel Through the Ages.* Salt Lake City: Steven & Wallis, 1945.

Jordan, Philip D. Introduction to *The Banditti of the Prairies,* by Edward Bonney. Norman, Okla.: U. of Oklahoma, 1963.

Journal of Discourses, vol. 1, 2, 4, 6.

Kelly, Charles, and Birney, Hoffman. *Holy Murder: The Story of Porter Rockwell.* New York: Minton, Balch, 1934.

McConkie, Bruce. *Mormon Doctrine*. Salt Lake City: Book-craft, 1958.

McIntosh, W. H. *History of Wayne County, New York, 1789-1877*. Philadelphia: Lippencott, n.d.

McKay, David O. *Gospel Ideals*. Salt Lake City: Deseret, 1953.

Millennial Star, vol. 15, 16, 17, 23.

Nibley, Hugh. *An Approach to the Book of Mormon*. Salt Lake City: Church of Jesus Christ of Latter-Day Saints, 1957.

Parry, Edwin F., comp. *Joseph Smith's Teachings*. Salt Lake City: Deseret, 1913.

Peterson, LaMar. *Problems in the Mormon Text*. Concord, Calif.: Pacific, 1957.

Peterson, Mark E. *Why Mormons Build Temples*. Salt Lake City: Deseret, n.d.

Pratt, Orson. *Absurdities of Materialism*. Liverpool: R. James for the Church of Jesus Christ of Latter-Day Saints, 1849.

Pratt, Parley P. *Key to the Science of Theology*. Salt Lake City: Deseret, 1883.

Richards, LeGrande. *A Marvelous Work and a Wonder*. Salt Lake City: Deseret, 1950.

Roberts, Brigham H. *A Comprehensive History of the Church of Jesus Christ of Latter-Day Saints*. Salt Lake City: Deseret, 1930.

-----. *Mormonism, Its Origin and History*, Independence, Mo.: Zion's, 1925.

Robertson, A. T. *Word Pictures in the New Testament*. Nashville: Broadman, 1943.

The Seer, p. 22.

Smith, Joseph Fielding. *Doctrines of Salvation*. Sermons of Joseph Fielding Smith compiled by Bruce R. McConkie. Salt Lake City: Bookcraft, 1954-56.

-----. *Gospel Doctrine*. 8th ed. Salt Lake City: Deseret, 1949.

-----. *The Progress of Man.* Salt Lake City: Genealogical
    Society of Utah, 1938.

Smith, Lucy Mack. *Biographical Sketches of Joseph Smith
    the Prophet and His Progenitors for Many Generations.*
    Published by Orson Pratt, Liverpool, 1853. Banned by
    Brigham Young. Rev. ed. published by Utah Church,
    1901.

Stanley, Reva. *Archer of Paradise.* Caldwell, Idaho: Caxton,
    1937.

Stout, Hosea. *On the Mormon Frontier: The Diary of Hosea
    Stout.* Salt Lake City: U. of Utah, 1964.

Talmage, James E. *The Articles of Faith.* Salt Lake City:
    Deseret, 1899, 1909.

-----. *The Great Apostasy: Considered in the Light of Scrip-
    tural and Secular History.* Salt Lake City: Deseret, 1909.

-----. *The Vitality of Mormonism.* Boston: Richard G.
    Badger, 1919.

Tanner, Jerald, and Tanner, Sandra. *Mormonism, Shadow
    or Reality.* Salt Lake City: Modern Microfilm, 1972.

Von Hagen, Victor Wolfgang. *The Aztec, Man and Tribe.*
    New York: Mentor, 1962.

Walters, Wesley P. *New Light on Mormon Origins.* La Mesa,
    Calif.: Utah Christian Tract Soc., 1967.

Werner, Morris Robert. *Brigham Young.* New York: Har-
    court, Brace, 1925.

Wheaton, Clarence L. *Historical Facts Concerning the
    Temple Lot.* Independence, Mo.: Board of Publications,
    Church of Christ (Temple Lot), 1954.

Widtsoe, John A. *Varieties of American Religion.* Chicago:
    Willet, Clark, 1936.